A New Species

A NEW SPECIES

Gender and Science in Science Fiction

Robin Roberts

University of Illinois Press
Urbana and Chicago

This book is printed on acid-free paper.

Library of Congress Cataloging-in-Publication Data

Roberts, Robin, 1957- .
    A new species : gender and science in science fiction / Robin
Roberts.
        p.   cm.
    Includes bibliographical references and index.
    ISBN 0-252-01983-0. — ISBN 0-252-06284-1 (pbk.)
    1. Science fiction, American—History and criticism. 2. Science
fiction, English—History and criticism. 3. Postmodernism
(Literature). 4. Feminism and literature. 5. Sex role in
literature. 6. Literature and science. 7. Utopias in literature.
8. Women and literature. I. Title.
PS374.S35R6   1993
813'.0876209—dc20   92-25385
                                                                CIP

To my parents

CONTENTS

ACKNOWLEDGMENTS

I am grateful to a number of people for their help in the completion of this book. First, I want to thank Nina Auerbach, whose own writing remains a model of feminist criticism at its best and whose encouragement to study the bizarre and unusual made my study of science fiction possible. She has helped and inspired me more than I can say. I am grateful to Pat Day and Judith Moffett, whose support and criticism of earlier versions of my manuscript were invaluable. I wish to thank the members of reading groups who discussed feminist theory and read versions of my work, especially Judith Johnston. The students in my science fiction classes have helped me clarify my thinking about science fiction. A Louisiana State University Summer Grant aided me in my completion of this project. Randall Knoper and Carl Freedman read sections of the manuscript. Michelle Massé and Elsie Michie read the entire manuscript and provided perceptive and constructive criticism. I am grateful to Ann Lowry and Terry Sears, at the University of Illinois Press, and to Elsie Michie for her commitment of considerable time and energy. Deborah Byrd, Randall Knoper, Kirk Curnutt, Laurie Drummond, Emily Toth, Rachel Kahn, Ruth Vance, Rosan Jordan, Frank De Caro, Matilda, Lucy, Tom, Bob C., and Peter Fischer provided support, encouragement, and much-needed distractions. Jane Donawerth supplied detailed suggestions that strengthened the argument. Keith Kelleman was there when I first began the project, and to him I am especially grateful. I wish also to thank my grandmother, Charlotte Moore, my sisters and brothers, Greg Pisklo, Gayle, Linda, David, Ricky, Laura, Roger, Kim, and Scott Roberts. The arguments from chapters 2 and 6 have appeared in earlier form in the *Journal of Popular Culture* and *Science-Fiction Studies.* An earlier version of chapter 5 appeared as "The Paradigm of *Frankenstein:* Reading Canopus in Argos in the Context of Science Fiction by Women" in *Extrapolation* 26 (1985): 16–23; used here with the permission of Kent State University Press. Thanks to Kit Kincade for creating the index.

INTRODUCTION

A New Species draws its title from Mary Shelley's *Frankenstein*[1] and argues that the new species—feminist science fiction—begins its life with that novel. It is an ambiguous and complex beginning, because in *Frankenstein* the female monster is never given a chance to live. However, even her nascent form is enough to inspire fear and dread that shapes subsequent science fiction aliens. This book analyzes the history of the female alien from her brief appearance in *Frankenstein* to her triumphant rule in contemporary feminist science fiction. The circuitous development of the female alien is lively and outré, and, among other things, requires critics to rethink the conventional readings of H. G. Wells's science fiction and to discover the wonderfully bizarre illustrations of female aliens in science fiction pulp magazines.

Until recently, feminist science fiction has been a critically neglected area of popular culture. While Natalie Rosinky's *Feminist Futures* explores the science fiction qualities of high art texts, Marleen Barr's *Alien to Femininity* astutely applies selected feminist theory to exemplary feminist science fiction texts, Nan Albinski's *Women's Utopias in British and American Fiction* provides a detailed history of idyllic feminist communities, and Sarah Lefanu's *Feminism and Science Fiction* considers science fiction as a genre and focuses on four feminist writers in depth, *A New Species* provides the first overview of science fiction from a feminist perspective. Placing feminist science fiction in a genealogy that runs from Shelley up to the postmodernist writers broadens our understanding of how what sounds like an oxymoron—feminism and science fiction—came to be a productive pairing. Too often, science fiction has been dismissed by critics and readers as fundamentally conservative and hence oppressive to women. As a careful reading of selected science fiction texts shows, however, the genre has always acknowledged the power of the feminine through its depiction of the female as alien. By isolating moments of science fiction's past, we can begin to see where, why, and how feminist science fiction was formed.

Feminist science fiction's long history may provide clues to how feminism itself can continue, even in inhospitable climates. Feminist science fiction can teach us to rethink traditional, patriarchal notions about science, reproduction, and gender. Only in science fiction can feminists imaginatively step outside the father's house and begin to look around. Feminist science fiction also provides lessons about popular culture and gender. Though popular culture is undoubtedly one site of oppression, it provides us with moments of resistance. We need to learn from postmodernist writers like Le Guin how and where to turn such insights to the service of feminism. If even so misogynistic a form as science fiction can be turned to feminist ends, then surely many other such conversions may be happening—and just as surely, many other areas of popular culture deserve the careful scrutiny of feminist critics. This study of science fiction shows that feminist critics should read popular culture carefully, that science fiction critics should appreciate the depth and range of feminist contributions to the genre, and that literary critics in general ought to look more carefully at the intersection of gender and popular literature.

Although the structure of this book is roughly chronological, the study relies on a sense of history, not as a clearly charted, linear worldview, but as a literary history in which texts have progenitors and ideas have lives of their own. I begin with Mary Shelley's *Frankenstein* and her neglected novel *The Last Man,* then proceed to explore the life of the female alien through contemporary feminist writers. Examining the images of women and science fiction explains why and how feminist science fiction emerged. The primary emphasis in this analysis is feminist, but I use other theories as well. Because science fiction critics have had to work so hard to justify study of the genre, science fiction criticism has not drawn sufficiently on the theories that have altered the way other genres are read. This study employs the insights of poststructuralists like Jean-François Lyotard and connects postmodernism and feminism. I draw on poststructuralist ideas about texts to license a reading of pulp science fiction art, a reading based on the work of Nina Auerbach, Bram Dijkstra, and others who have explored the relation between the visual arts and literary texts. I then use new ideas about the practice of science, pioneered by critics like Evelyn Fox Keller and Donna Haraway, to read feminist utopias and science fiction by focusing on the implications of science as story for feminist revisionists. Doris Lessing's science fiction is explored for its synthesis of issues raised in feminist utopias and science fiction. Her use of innovative narrative form prepares for the structural and stylistic innovations of postmodern feminist science fiction writers like Ursula K. Le Guin. Understanding feminist science fiction's development from Shelley to postmodernist writers will provide science fiction critics with a more complete picture of the genre and feminist critics with a new genre to study.

Science fiction is customarily thought of as a masculine genre, although some of its most highly regarded practitioners are women. On the surface, many of the conventions of science fiction appear to be unabashedly and irredeemably misogynistic, but science fiction by male writers often presents so extreme a version of misogyny that the reader can find a strong case for feminism in the texts. More than other genres, science fiction is obsessed with the figure of Woman: not only as potential sexual partner but, more interestingly, as alien, as ruler, and as mother. From these character types, women science fiction writers create an empowering portrayal of female strength. Women writers appropriate the female alien, utopias, and the woman ruler and transform them into feminist models. These feminist narratives range from conventional structures to the complex strategies employed by postmodernist feminist science fiction writers. Paradoxically, the genre's obsession with Woman as evil allows women writers to subvert the overtly sexist paradigms of science fiction. This book situates feminist science fiction in a tradition that explains how and why women writers have been able to use science fiction for explicitly feminist narratives.[2]

To understand why Doris Lessing and other women writers have turned to so seemingly uncongenial a genre as science fiction, their readers must first understand the conventions of the genre and its ideological implications. As its name suggests, from its very beginning science fiction has been associated with science, and the genre does reflect and reify cultural assumptions about science and scientists. While my focus here is not on a history of science or on a history of women, I use ideas about both science and gender to explain the genesis of feminist science fiction. Like Jane Donawerth, whose insightful article on utopian science provides an overview of the parallels between feminist theories of science and women science fiction writers' imaginary sciences, I am primarily a literary critic drawing on the wealth of feminist criticism of science.

Despite what cultural myth tells us about the objective "truths" of science, science too is shaped by myths, by fabrications, fabulations, and stories, as Lyotard explains.[3] This poststructuralist view of science was first articulated by Donna Haraway, who in her analysis of primatology explains that "scientific practice is above all a story-telling practice in the sense of historically specific practices of interpretation and testimony" (*Primate Vi-*

sions 4).[4] Unfortunately, science is a storytelling practice conducted primarily by men. In "Is the Subject of Science Sexed?" for example, Luce Irigaray critiques scientific imperialism and argues that the subject of science is sexed in a number of disciplines, from economics to linguistics to biology. Through its blind sexism, science imposes a false universality, what Lyotard calls a "grand narrative." As historians of science like Stephen Jay Gould show, science's grand narrative has been used to justify the oppression of subordinate groups, including women.

Because science wields power as a source of legitimacy for ideology,[5] women need to pay attention to the discourse of science. Vivian Gornick insists that "scientists do what writers do" and stresses that, in the lives of actual female scientists, "art, science, feminism . . . came to seem metaphors for each other" (38–39). This symbiosis is what science fiction can offer feminists. Using the tropes of science fiction, feminist writers reconstruct science to provide a critique of and an imaginative alternative to real-life science, a field still inhospitable to women. Gornick does not find that women practice science differently than men do, but she claims that practices are changing for women scientists because of feminism as an idea and a movement (146).

Feminist literary critics are not alone in their critique of science, for feminist historians of science have also made excursions against the edifice of science and drawn connections between feminism and the practice of science. Significantly, some of them use feminist science fiction to criticize and explain traditional science. For example, Haraway begins and ends part 1 of her frequently reprinted essay "Animal Sociology and a Natural Economy of the Body Politic" with quotations from Marge Piercy's *Woman on the Edge of Time* that stress the visionary and collective nature of revising science. Like other readers of this female utopia, Haraway takes seriously Piercy's revisioning of science and uses it to frame her argument critiquing traditional primatology. Similarly, her book *Primate Visions* concludes with a discussion of Octavia Butler's science fiction and its parallels to scientific discourses about primatology. Through her discussion of Butler and other women science fiction writers, Haraway acknowledges the radical possibilities of science fiction as a genre and its similarity to scientific narrative. "Science fiction writers also stake their craft on the premise that knowledge is fundamentally political; i.e., dialectically constituted by and constitutive of social possibility" (111). Elsewhere, Haraway explains how science fiction mirrors science: "The sciences have always had a utopian character. In their efforts to *describe* the world, to understand how it actually 'works,' scientists simultaneously search out the limits of possible worlds" ("Animal Sociology" 80). Not only are science and science fiction parallel, but science fiction shapes the possibilities of scientific vision. "What determines a 'good' story in the natural and social sciences," Haraway declares, "is partly decided by available social visions of these possible worlds" ("Animal Sociology" 80).

Underlying this feminist transformation of science is a recognition of the socially constructed category of gender. By exposing the rigid binarism of gender divisions and proposing alternatives to parceling science and feminism into two neat piles, feminist science fiction deconstructs science and traditional science fiction, which both contain a gender split between "hard" and "soft" science. This distinction is used, often unself-consciously, by scientists, writers, and readers of science fiction. The natural sciences are categorized as hard because they are ostensibly more objective and rigorous, while the social sciences are depicted as soft because, in this construction, they are supposedly more subjective and easier to master. These categories are coded through gender, as Sandra Harding points out in *The Science Question in Feminism.*[6]

In science fiction, "hard" refers to fiction that focuses on technology where the fiction's hardware is scrupulously accurate: nothing in a piece of hard science fiction contradicts known scientific facts, at least the facts known at the time of the work's creation. Often even the plot of a hard science fiction book revolves around a particular scientific fact, as in novels by H. G. Wells, Robert Heinlein, and Hal Clement. Soft science fiction, on the other hand, tends to focus on the social sciences: psychology, sociology, even parapsychology. Many soft science fiction writers expand the social sciences by creating and embracing an imaginary science known as psionics, which includes telekinesis, telepathy, and teleportation (Lefanu 88–89). Although there are male soft science fiction writers, most hard science fiction is written by men, while women write soft science fiction almost exclusively. Feminist utopias frequently reject hard technology altogether (Schweickart). The distinction itself carries overt valuation: many science fiction writers, critics, and readers stress scientific accuracy and plausibility and see soft science fiction writers as weakening the field by diluting its true purpose of hard scientific extrapolation.

The distinction between hard and soft science, however, turns out to be difficult to maintain, particularly when hard science is practiced in relation to reproduction. For example, although new technologies involving human reproduction are clearly hard science, that is, they rely on machinery and biology, these technologies have been characterized as soft, in part because of their immediate implications for social organization and also, perhaps, because of their association with women. Over the past several years, the Associated Press has released a number of articles that read as if they were soft science fiction stories. "Unfertilized Embryo Grew" was reported in the prestigious British weekly *Nature* in 1983. And on March 25, 1986, an article entitled "Is Sex Necessary? Evolutionists Are Perplexed" appeared in the Science Times section of the *New York Times*. The writer surveyed theories about evolution and concluded: "None of these theories is flattering to the males of any species. At best males are portrayed as useful sources of genetic variety. One theory justifies males as storehouses of redundant information that females can draw on, if necessary, to repair damaged genes. Another describes sex as a sort of disease, with males as mere agents of persuasion" (C11). An AP story picked up by the Bridgewater, N.J., *Courier-News* on July 17, 1986, reported that scientists claim all human beings can be traced back to a single female ancestor (A3). Scientific research on breaking down and redefining gender roles makes the soft science fiction written by feminists seem predictive and certainly hard in the sense of accurately reflecting the current state of science.

Unfortunately, even though these new reproductive narratives are narratives about women, women usually do not write these stories. Women cannot control scientific narratives because, although they are frequently its subject, they are largely excluded from the practice of science. Through feminist science fiction, however, women can write narratives about science. With its imaginative possibilities, science fiction provides women opportunities denied them in the real world. In their revisions of traditional myths, feminist writers can use science fiction to create the feminist fairy tales that are needed to counteract the misogynistic stories of our culture (Rowe). In science fiction, the magical powers that enable the miraculous plots of fairy tales are replaced with a science that is often just as mysterious to characters as a fairy godmother's magic wand. Because of our culture's tendency to look to science for solutions and cultural progress, science fiction often inhabits the same imaginative frame as fairy tales. Feminist science fiction also calls into question the legitimization of patriarchy through conventional science and focuses on—and tries to change—the gendered categories and myths that shape the world of science. Unlike traditional science fiction, which perpetuates the gendered cultural myths of science, feminist science fiction works to deconstruct these myths and to refashion them into myths that authorize the experience of women. Thanks to feminist writers, women in science fiction do have a science, or even sciences, of their own.

The danger of leaping too quickly to a dismissal of science as magic has long been an accepted tenet of science fiction, as in Arthur C. Clarke's Third Law, "Any sufficiently advanced technology is indistinguishable from magic" (Pournelle 245). John W. Campbell, for many years the influential and well-respected editor of *Astounding,* expressed a similar view when he wrote, "Science is magic that works" (qtd. in Bretnor 40). These aphorisms point to science fiction's emphasis on perspective. The depiction of magic as a science seen from an uninformed point of view allows women science fiction writers to draw on a long tradition of feminine power, the tradition of witches and magic. Witches in Europe from the fourteenth to the seventeenth centuries employed the scientific method, while the efforts of medical men during the same time period were "anti-empirical." Ehrenreich and English point to the number of drugs tested by "years of use" that were later rediscovered by doctors, drugs such as belladonna, ergot, and digitalis. Even more important than her development of certain drugs were the witchhealer's methods: "She relied on her senses rather than on faith or doctrine, she believed in trial and error, cause and effect" (14). In contrast, doctors followed the dictates of the Church, which "discredited the value of the material world, and had a profound distrust of the senses" (14). The conflict between women healers and male scientists was a struggle about methods as well as for the control of a profession. Female healers offered what might be called "alternate science" to the ill, but their methods were dismissed as magic and condemned as religiously and scientifically suspect. As the history of witches demonstrates, science becomes magic—hence, dangerous—when practiced by women. In this context, the word "science" refers to the gender of the practitioner rather than a difference in method.

Male and female science fiction writers alike use and question the historical distinction between magic and science, but while hard science fiction writers usually reveal that what seemed to be magic was really science, feminist writers radically undermine the distinction between magic and science. In science fiction by male writers, magical powers are usually depicted as evil and corrupt and the female scientist is often taunted with the cry of "witch," as are the Bene Gesserit in Frank Herbert's *Dune.* In his Hugo and Nebula award-winning novel, Herbert resuscitates the medieval condemnation of witches as satanic. At the end of *Dune,* the hero, Paul, becomes the Emperor and rejects the Reverend Mother of the Bene Gesserit, even though she gave him the first indication of his powers and in fact was, through her breeding program, indirectly responsible for his birth. Despite his debt to this sisterhood of witches, Paul dismisses feminine power and excludes women from his government. Similarly, Philip José Farmer creates a race of witches known as the *lalitha* in "The Lovers." Like Herbert, Farmer provides the female aliens with magical powers but subordinates the race to them. Because the *lalitha* need human males to reproduce and because bearing young kills the mother, these witches are left to the mercy of mankind.

In feminist science fiction, the figure of the witch and many other overtly sexist tropes are recovered for feminist purposes. While male science fiction writers characterize witches as magical and evil, female writers depict magic as valorizing for women and as a legitimate science. Nineteenth-century science fiction novelists from Shelley onward redefine female magic as science, making women doubly powerful as they claim science for themselves and resist the narrow definition of science offered by patriarchal society. Feminist science fiction develops not only from a need to reclaim and reimagine science but also from a series of literary paradigms first codified by Shelley and carried through popular science fiction of the later nineteenth century which then became feminist science fiction. For example, in her Witch World series, Andre Norton depicts a world in which women rule beneficently through magic powers traditionally associated with witches, such as the ability to foretell the future, to communicate telepathically, to speak to animals, and to move through space using only the power of their minds. These powers are redefined in science fiction as psionics, a term first coined by John Campbell. In Norton's novels, as in many other works of feminist science fiction, psionics wielded by women topples male-dominated traditionally technological societies.

Psionics has been appropriated by women writers, just as they have appropriated the idea of witches, for feminist ends. Yet the adaptation occurs in the context of science fiction rather than fantasy. Feminist science fiction writers provide plausible explanations for magical powers. For example, in her Hugo Award–winning *Dreamsnake,* Vonda McIntyre's female protagonist, Snake, has the witchlike ability to communicate with animals. As Snake carefully explains, however, her ability results from a program of advanced psychological training, making the skill potentially available to any of the characters in the novel. By emphasizing the scientific qualities of soft science and the magical qualities of hard science, writers like McIntyre overcome the dichotomy between valid hard science and invalid soft science.

Nineteenth-century science fiction begins the division of science into hard and soft categories and firmly grounds that division in terms of gender. Throughout nineteenth-century science fiction, female aliens draw upon the power of women to reproduce and the power of an alternative science. Through the figure of the female alien, science fiction writers affirm the essential otherness of Woman and the threat that she poses to patriarchal society. The female alien is at her worst and her most powerful in female dystopias, which posit all-female worlds or worlds run by women: here Woman appears as evolution gone awry. The writers of these dystopian worlds evoke Darwin to suggest the awful possibility of Woman (a separate species in this formulation) supplanting and then disposing of mankind. In this regard, science fiction differs from the mainstream in its depiction of Woman as devolution, Woman as the kind of evolutionary regression also chronicled in nineteenth-century painting by Bram Dijkstra.

This tension and anxiety about the New Woman manifests itself differently in science fiction than in mainstream art. In science fiction, the myths that appear in nineteenth-century art turn into monsters, but when they are associated with science, monsters like the sphinx and Medusa appear more formidable and less evil. In these fictions, women have powers that can threaten male dominance: the first is their ability to reproduce; the second, to use magic, an alternative to hard science. These powers define the figure of the female alien and enable her to rule societies and even worlds. The female alien can be represented ambiguously: in general, male science fiction writers depict her as a figure of horror, while female science fiction writers appropriate her as a symbol of strength and empowerment. The notion of the feminine as alien and uncontrollable is a venerable science fiction trope that can be traced to the dismembered female monster in *Frankenstein* and her descendants in novels by Edward G. Bulwer-Lytton, H. G. Wells, and Walter Besant. While the female aliens in nineteenth-century science fiction *are* demonic, their demonic nature is developed under the particularly compelling aegis of science (Auerbach, *Woman and the Demon*). The female alien is often nonhumanoid; nevertheless, her specifically feminine traits, such as mothering, nurturing, passivity, and sexual attractiveness to human males, suggest that this figure represents human women.

The female alien reveals anxieties about woman's power as mother. In the nineteenth-century, as sex and reproduction became the province of scientific study, women became increasingly feared as the source of evolution or devolution. Writers worried that the "wrong" groups of people were reproducing, while upper- and middle-class white women were shirking their duty of maintaining the human race. Motherhood became an ambivalent source of power for women and an obsession in science fiction from the nineteenth century to the twentieth. As I argue, a fascination with the process of reproduction dominates science fiction, beginning with *Frankenstein,* which first introduced science as a male substitute for the female biological power of reproducing. The history of science fiction contradicts Lefanu's assertion that a mother is "that rarest of all beings in the world of science fiction" (15–16). She may be right about the scarcity of *human* mothers, but mothering is frequently represented through aliens. Traditional science fiction like "The Lovers" reveals that mothers and mothering characterize women as alien, threatening, central, and powerful. These pejorative descriptions, however, have been transformed by women writers into pictures of feminine strength. Science fiction's emphasis on mothering makes the genre particularly worthy of feminist scrutiny.

The reduction of woman to reproductive organ described by Simone de Beauvoir and other feminist critics explains why both male and female science fiction writers are fascinated by the female alien. Through their reproductive capacity, women have the power to threaten patriarchy, which explains both the fear of women and their oppression. The power of reproduction makes women essential to the human race, but they also control patriarchal lineage because the child is incontrovertibly only the woman's. In her award-winning study of motherhood, *Of Woman Born,* Adrienne Rich explains, "There is much to suggest that the male mind has always been haunted by the force of the idea of *dependence on a woman for life itself,* the son's constant effort to assimilate, compensate for or deny the fact that he is 'of woman born'" (xiii). Rich defines motherhood as "the biological potential or capacity to bear and nourish human life" and the cultural reaction to motherhood as "the magical power invested in women by men, whether in the form of Goddess-worship or the fear of being controlled and overwhelmed by women" (xv). Her interpretation of this gender dynamic is underscored by Julia Kristeva's description of the archaic and all-powerful mother from whom the human infant must separate: "Fear of the archaic mother turns out to be fear of her generative power" (77). Feminist science fiction tames the figure of the archaic mother, a figure that appears in Doris Lessing's Canopus in Argos series, in which a space empire becomes a mother to the entire human race.

A New Species comprises an alternative history of science fiction, one that focuses particularly on issues of gender. Consequently, familiar texts like *Frankenstein* and *The Time Machine* are considered along with less well known nineteenth-century feminist utopias. This book contains the first discussion of feminism and pulp science fiction art, a defense of Doris Lessing's science fiction, and the first discussion of postmodernism and feminist science fiction. Each chapter isolates an important moment in the development of science fiction's treatment of gender. The thread that runs throughout is the depiction of woman as alien and the appropriation of science fiction tropes for feminist purposes.

The historicity of feminist recovery of the female alien is examined in chapter 1, which charts science fiction's obsession with woman through the female alien, who first appears in Shelley's *Frankenstein,* reemerges in *The Last Man,* and then reappears in the popular Victorian novels *The Coming Race* by Bulwer-Lytton, *The Revolt of Man* by Besant, and *The Time Machine* by Wells. More so than any other science fiction texts, *Frankenstein* and *The Last Man* reveal ambivalence about reproduction as a source of power for women. While the female alien is threatening by herself, when she dominates a society as a ruler, as she does in Bulwer-Lytton's, Besant's, and Wells's novels, she is doubly threatening to patriarchy. Studying these early fictions reveals the roots of contemporary feminist science fiction.

Chapter 2 deals with a neglected and unique aspect of science fiction, namely, its visual depictions of woman. This chapter follows the female alien/ruler into the pulp science fiction magazines of the 1940s and 1950s. In these popular magazines, named for the cheap, pulpy quality of their paper, the female alien gains renewed vigor in pictorial representations that vividly demonstrate the anxieties about gender represented more subtly in the prose. These magazines provide the clearest and most revealing images of women's strength, and they are also worth studying because of the connections between the pulps and contemporary science fiction. The cover art and cover stories reveal that the female alien and the woman ruler were transformed in the pages of the pulp science fiction magazines in a way that rendered them available for feminist appropriation.

While the first two chapters focus primarily on the feminists' legacy from the male writers, the third chapter moves the study from a consideration of misogynistic patterns to the way feminists recover these patterns. Chapter 3 explores the female utopia, a feminist response to patriarchy. Feminist utopias represent a midpoint between the early science fiction dystopias and later feminist science fiction. Through the notion of a utopia, a world that is both perfect and nonexistent—"nowhere," as the word's roots suggest—feminist writers create a separate space for women. From Mary E. Bradley Lane's *Mizora: A Prophecy* and Charlotte Perkins Gilman's *Herland* to later feminist utopias such as James Schmitz's *Witches of Karres,* Dorothy Bryant's *Kin of Ata Are Waiting for You,* Ursula K. Le Guin's *Left Hand of Darkness,* Joanna Russ's *Female Man,* Suzy McKee Charnas's *Motherlines,* and Marge Piercy's *Woman on the Edge of Time,* feminist utopias enact the strategy of separatism. This chapter demonstrates the ways in which, in the nineteenth and twentieth centuries, the emphasis on science and the female alien can be subverted to create all-female worlds that challenge our gendered notions of reality. Scientific advances have enabled twentieth-century feminist writers to expand their use of the art/psionics model as an alternative science. Technological advances in reproduction such as in vitro fertilization have made the magical powers of witches and goddesses seem more possible, while research on the brain indicates at least the possibility of new mental powers.[7] In the twentieth century, soft science has begun to be legitimated; thus, feminist science fiction has become more acceptable.

In chapter 4, I discuss novels that emphasize equality, not only of men and women, but also between races. While the feminist utopia provides an effective setting in which to criticize patriarchal science, it is limited by its separatist demarcation. Feminist science fiction stresses character development, which feminist utopias, because of their emphasis on community, cannot. Feminist science fiction has more room for ambiguity and difference than the utopias do. This shift reflects the shift within feminism itself, from a monolithic white heterosexual middle-class feminism to feminisms, or from women's rights to issues of gender, race, and class. These fictions rely on four patterns: male science versus female magic, alternative science and art, versions of the Demeter myth, and women and science in a post-apocalyptic world. All these patterns appear in Andre Norton's *Witch World,* Joan D. Vinge's *Snow Queen,* Suzette Haden Elgin's *Communipath Worlds,* James Tiptree's *Up the Walls of the World,* Vonda McIntyre's *Dreamsnake,* "Cassandra" by C. J. Cherryh, and "The Heat Death of the Universe" by Pamela Zoline.

Chapter 5 explores the example of Doris Lessing, who draws on postmodernism and the female alien/ruler in her epic series Canopus in Argos. Lessing's science fiction deals with all the issues raised in preceding chapters, including the move from feminist utopias to more complex feminist science fiction. Lessing addresses the conflict between masculine science and feminine magic and resolves the split by deconstructing the binarism and incorporating a feminist utopia into her science fiction series. She uses science fiction to comment on human history, particularly the hideous treatment of witches, and she valorizes the power of language and art to challenge patriarchal society. Scrutinizing the way that the qualities of science fiction insinuate themselves into Lessing's earlier novels and the eruption of the science fiction elements into the Canopus in Argos series reveals the attraction and utility of science fiction for women writers.

Finally, in chapter 6, I look at the ways in which a contemporary phenomenon—postmodernism—is drawn into the discussion of science and language in feminist science fiction. Employing new deconstructive theories, feminist science fiction writers use science fiction concepts and cultural theories to challenge patriarchal assumptions even more forcefully than their predecessors did. Through their postmodernist feminist science fictions, Le Guin (*Always Coming Home*), Joan Slonczewski (*A Door into Ocean*), Sheila Finch (*Triad*), and Margaret Atwood (*The Handmaid's Tale*) demonstrate the similarity and combined power of feminism and postmodernism. They do so by repeating the patterns of woman as alien, seen in earlier fictions, but they complicate the presentation through narrative structures that draw attention to the way language can be used to oppress and confine women.

As feminist science fiction demonstrates, the misogynistic paradigms of science fiction provide a starting point for an entirely different vision of the future. The feminist point of view self-consciously reclaims the figures of woman as alien and woman as ruler and denies any simple, binary oppositions. By focusing on the special position of women as reproducers of the human race and its culture, women writers can imagine a world based on the female values described by feminist psychologists like Carol Gilligan and Mary Belenky. Although it relies heavily on the traditions of science fiction, feminist science fiction consists of more than a mere inversion of science fiction tropes. Apparently misogynistic paradigms of the female alien and the female ruler provide a starting point for an entirely different journey to a future shaped by a feminist itinerary. Through the patterns of science fiction, women writers self-consciously create not just a room of their own but also worlds and even universes of their own. Through all-female worlds or nonsexist worlds, women writers present blueprints for a feminist design of society at the same time that they re-view and reevaluate the whole of human history through a feminist lens. Science fiction enables women writers to criticize the past as well as provide for the future. Weaving together the strands of woman as scientist/witch/mother, these writers threaten and transform conventional notions of science. Through the traditional settings of science fiction, writers present feminist alternatives to male science and to patriarchal societies. Le Guin has said that "science fiction is the mythology of the modern world" (*Language of the Night* 73). It is a mythology now transformed by women writers.

Notes

1. Victor Frankenstein imagines "a new species would bless me as its creator and source" (Shelley 52).

2. Traditional science fiction's misogyny is emphasized by the reaction of shock and surprise occasioned by the science fiction of feminist writers like Doris Lessing. Her sudden transformation from a "realistic writer to a cosmic visionary" seems inexplicable to the *New York Times* writer who worries that "readers and critics now fear that she is tumbling from the pedestal that they erected for her" (Hazelton 21). At issue is not just Lessing's position but that of all women writing science fiction.

3. Lyotard explains that science tells *stories* and is shaped by the *grand récit* of the Enlightenment, a universalizing story now being called into question. He cites P. B. Medwar, who "has stated that '*having ideas* is the scientist's highest accomplishment,' that there is no 'scientific method,' and that a scientist is before anything else a person who 'tells stories'" (Lyotard 60).

4. This view of science was first depicted in Haraway's "Animal Sociology."

5. The authors of *Not in Our Genes,* a widely acclaimed analysis of biological determinism, point out that "science is now the source of legitimacy for ideology" (Lewontin et al. 29).

6. Similarly, Sherry Turkle describes two types of computer programming: hard and soft mastery of the computer are gender-linked styles (101–5).

7. On January 17, 1984, it was reported on the PBS series *Nova* that "for over a decade, the U.S. government has also been funding psychic research at SRI [Society for Psychical Research]" ("The Case for ESP," transcript no. 1101).

ONE

Gender in Nineteenth-Century Science Fiction: The Female Alien and the Woman Ruler

Although modern science fiction begins with a woman writer, Mary Shelley, misogyny runs as a constant and central thread through its fabric.[1] This chapter explores the metamorphic reproductive myths that emerge from Shelley's science fiction and shows how her novels have led, first, to a codification of the larger culture's depiction of Woman as Other in negative portraits of female aliens and women rulers and, nascently, to feminist appropriation of these figures. These two character types appear frequently in science fiction, but they appear in their most negative and most compelling forms in the genre's modern beginnings in the nineteenth century. The female alien can be a human woman, rendered alien by her femininity to a male character, a gendered being from another planet, or, as in *Frankenstein,* a female creature. A woman ruler is a character or group of women who dominate or run a society or world, as does the disease PLAGUE, personified by Shelley in *The Last Man.*

Frankenstein poses peculiar problems for a critic because it has been transformed from a text into a cultural myth. My feminist interpretation of the text traces but one thread of a complex weave that has supplied innumerable critics with material for diametrically opposed readings.[2] I do not attempt a "totalizing" reading of the text but instead suggest how the text raises issues about the feminine in ways that shape later science fiction.[3]

Frankenstein should be read in concert with Shelley's long-neglected *Last Man.* Both texts focus on the female power to reproduce, a power allied with science and with writing itself. The obsession with reproduction shapes Shelley's depiction of woman as alien and her description of art as a redemptive force. Her science fiction novels encompass what is later divided into hard and soft science and science fiction. This reconciliation of oppositions in Shelley's science fiction fuels the divergent masculinist and feminist traditions in subsequent science fiction, as the following chapters demonstrate. Shelley's generative juxtaposition also helps to explain the recurrent fascination with the best-known science fiction story, the story of Frankenstein and his creation.

Although they use male protagonists, Shelley's novels illuminate how science fiction subversively prepares for feminist revision. I would call *Frankenstein* and *The Last Man* codedly feminine, by which I mean a process whereby an author forced by cultural, literary, or personal constraints explores a singularly feminine dilemma using a male character as a stand-in, or cover.[4] A coded feminine reading often explains the appeal for feminist readers of an apparently womanless text.[5] Like many other male characters in science fiction, Shelley's male protagonists face essentially feminine situations and dilemmas. Woman writers like Shelley also use male characters as stand-ins for women even when they want to discuss problems of concern to women: sexism, reproduction, isolation from professions. Feminist readings of *Frankenstein* and *The Last Man* show that Shelley's science fiction is centrally concerned with femininity.

More so than any other science fiction texts, *Frankenstein* and *The Last Man* reveal ambivalence about reproduction as a source of power for women. Shelley simultaneously depicts reproduction as an apocalyptic force, a force that can level patriarchal civilizations, and also as a self-destructive means of wielding power. In *Frankenstein* and, to a lesser degree, *The Last Man,* Shelley depicts mothering, creating and nurturing offspring, as a source of pain and vulnerability, as it was for Demeter when she lost Persephone, but also as a source of anger and destruction, as when Demeter creates the first winter to mark her loss.[6]

While this story shapes both of Shelley's science fiction novels, the pattern is clearest in *Frankenstein.* Because the central narrative of the text focuses on Frankenstein's psychological conflict with his creation, critics have interpreted the novel as concerned with mothering. Like Demeter's, Frankenstein's anguish at being separated from his creation and the creation's sorrow are reflected in the winter landscape that pervades the book. The Arctic frames the narrative; the turning point, where the monster asks for a mate and Frankenstein begins to create her, occurs in the snow and ice of the Alps. The Arctic snow and ice is a landscape perfectly suited to reflect Frankenstein and the creation's torment at the sundering of their relationship, as the first winter represents Demeter's anguish at being separated from Persephone.

Frankenstein's setting of snow and ice also recalls Demeter's inability to rescue her daughter: in the myths of patriarchal culture, feminine power is the power to thwart but not to act. Similarly, Frankenstein cannot act when his creature begins murdering his family and friends; instead, he passively waits. At the moment of conception, Frankenstein describes himself as "'timid as a love-sick girl'" (Mellor 100). Appropriately, then, Shelley uses ice and snow to emphasize Frankenstein's femininity, which is demonstrated not only by his ability to reproduce but also by his sensitivity and passivity, stereotypically feminine traits.[7] Ellen Moers has suggested the importance of *Frankenstein* as "distinctly a *woman's* mythmaking on the subject of birth" because of the novel's emphasis on "the trauma of the afterbirth" (142). In this interpretation, Frankenstein's and the monster's sufferings are those of a mother and her rejected child, transmuted from the suffering Shelley endured after her own miscarriages.

In their transformation into the realm of science, Shelley's personal sufferings produced a response that lasted for generations. Shelley was well versed in the scientific knowledge of her day, and her critique of masculinist science was thorough. She "illustrated the potential lures of scientific hubris and at the same time illustrated the cultural biases inherent in any conception of science and the scientific method that rested on a gendered definition of nature as female" (Mellor 89). The tremendous popularity of the novel suggests that Shelley struck a cultural nerve, a sense of unease about reproduction and mothering, especially science's potential to change reproduction. In this reading of the novel, Frankenstein's travails are those of an ambivalent mother as well as those of the transgressor of the feminine power of reproduction (Mellor 100–101). "His profound desire to reunite with his dead mother [is] a desire that can be fulfilled only by Victor's becoming himself a mother" (Mellor 122).

While feminist critics are able to see general issues about mothering in *Frankenstein,* they miss another codedly feminine plot because they assume the usual opposition between science and the feminine. Approaching the novel as a feminist reader of science fiction allows me to make visible another narrative, one not centered on the biological. In my reading, Frankenstein himself is a codedly feminine character and his story is that of a scientist who practices alternative, or "female," science. While I agree with Mellor that Shelley criticizes gendered science, I argue that Frankenstein functions not only as the crazed scientist who wants to control nature but also as the scientist who adopts a feminized position by practicing an unconventional science. After all, it is Victor who gives birth to an "abortion" (*Frankenstein* 210).

Erasmus Darwin, whose work Shelley knew, at one point "attributed all monstrous births to the female" (Mellor 98). The creation of the monster itself is shrouded in mystery and magic; the sources of Frankenstein's inspiration are the alchemists, practitioners of a magic that serves as an alternative to the science Frankenstein is supposed to study. Alchemists like Agrippa are linked with the femininity of creating life (Thornburg 82). Chemistry becomes a science in the nineteenth century, so alchemy then becomes defined as feminine in relation to modern, masculine science. Despite his father's and other scientists' disparaging remarks, Frankenstein's study of and enthusiasm for alchemists result in his act of creation. While many men practiced alchemy, in the context of the gendering of hard and soft science, alchemists of whatever sex practiced a "feminine" soft science. Frankenstein, then, practices an alternative science, but its particulars cast him as a potential bridge between hard and soft science.

The novel also demonstrates dangers associated with practicing alternative science. Witchlike, Frankenstein works in secret: he fears the ridicule of scientists at the university and hopes to transcend the limitations of the scientific method. Prefiguring the female prophets in Piercy's *Woman on the Edge of Time* and Lessing's *Four-Gated City,* Frankenstein constantly worries that he will be imprisoned and ridiculed if he announces his discovery. Rather than expose himself to imprisonment and ridicule, he allows a female servant to be executed and then unconvincingly rationalizes his silence: "my purposed avowal died away on my lips. Thus I might proclaim myself a madman" (85). Because Frankenstein is unable to handle the responsibilities of mothering his creation, the female servant, his fiancée, the creature's mate, and Frankenstein all die. Through Frankenstein's story, Shelley valorizes the female power of reproduction and depicts it as the most dangerous power in the world. Its misuse causes the death of all the women in the novel, suggesting that, paradoxically, reproduction can function as both a source of creativity and a source of destruction for women.

Through science fiction, writers like Shelley demonstrate another way to criticize science. *Frankenstein* can be read as an exposé of the way writing affects science. Frankenstein's account of his experiment, a scientific narrative, can be used to delegitimize the voice and perspective of the object of study—in this case, the monster. The narrator's (Walton's) and Frankenstein's accounts differ completely from the monster's, which we receive much later in the novel. But once we read the creature's narrative, we realize how we have been manipulated by Frankenstein's discourse. As Jean Rhys wrote *Wide Sargasso Sea* to provide Charlotte Brontë's Bertha Mason with a voice, so feminist science fiction writers like Mary E. Bradley Lane and Vonda McIntyre adopt the plot and setting of *Frankenstein* to give voice to feminist alternatives to traditional science.

One feminist strategy is to persuade males to act differently; in this regard, Walton's conversion is central to the plot. He opens the novel as a macho explorer, hoping to "tread a land never before imprinted by the foot of man" (15), but converts from a scientist-explorer to a writer-storyteller who addresses a female audience, his sister. When Frankenstein dies and the monster flees, the ship breaks free from the ice, allowing Walton and his crew to return to civilization. Their renunciation of exploration signals his conversion to a less macho position—he proves willing to listen to others and has decided to return to feminine society, represented by his sister. The overt address of the novel to a female audience supports a codedly feminine reading of *Frankenstein*. Through the novel's narrative construction, Shelley affirms its feminist focus; the narration consists of journals and letters, traditionally a form accessible to and used by woman writers. Shelley clearly distinguishes her feminist attitude toward art from the Romantic conventions of high art: her novels are a domesticated version of the same themes that obsessed the Romantics, but her presentation—prose in the form of letters and journals—foregrounds a feminine identification.

The form of *Frankenstein* is reborn in feminist science fiction. Contemporary woman writers like Lessing use journals and letters to stress, as Shelley does, the importance of art and of the writer who preserves the events of the story and who shapes the narrative. The multiplicity of narrational perspectives denies the possibility of an absolute, authoritarian point of view and instead emphasizes a more relativistic, perhaps feminine (and, by extrapolation, eventually feminist), narration (Mellor 125). Frankenstein's dilemma could well be used as one of the test situations for Gilligan's reexamination of the Kohlberg test for moral development. Although Frankenstein struggles to impose his order on the narrative, his omniscient and traditional narration is undercut by the other perspectives, particularly the monster's often poignant account of his abandonment. In combination with the focus on reproduction, the narration's fragmentation assumes greater political significance: *Frankenstein*'s plot points to a resolution of the conflict between science and art by suggesting the primacy of domestic art over science. Shelley's privileging of social art contrasts strikingly with standard Romantic notions of high art. Rather than the solitary poet as redeemer, Shelley posits a collaborative, feminine art reflected in the journals and narratives, which allow a number of voices to be heard. The effect of writing is also stressed through Victor's death; without the narration, his achievements would be buried with him in the Arctic.

Besides providing a central paradigm for the female science fiction tradition, Shelley's novel also inspires the masculine tradition's misogyny. In the Greek myth, Demeter's love for her daughter is unalloyed and she is willing to do anything to have her daughter returned to her. However, Frankenstein's creation is conceived through science, not love; Frankenstein's parental feelings are mixed. The effect of hard science, especially its emphasis on distance, objectivity, and control of the experiment, can be seen in Frankenstein's hate and fear of the female he creates for the monster. Although she never breathes, this female monster comes alive as Frankenstein imagines the tremendous and dangerous powers of the male monster augmented by femininity. In disgust and fear, "trembling with passion," he murders the female creature, tearing her body "to pieces" (159). He sees her as a rival, his equal, who could produce a race of creatures: "She might become ten thousand times more malignant than her mate and, delight, for its own sake, in murder and wretchedness" (158). Through her, "a race of devils would be propagated upon the earth who might make the very existence of the species of man a condition precarious and full of terror" (159).

As in many later works of science fiction, it is the female alien's ability to reproduce that makes her so threatening to the male protagonist and to patriarchal society. In *Frankenstein,* reproduction is depicted as "a filthy process" (156) in which Victor must engage when he undertakes to reproduce a mate for the creature. At the same time that he fears her reproductive capacity, Frankenstein is terrified by the possibility of the female's independence. As he contemplates her powers, he imagines that the creature "might turn with disgust from him [the male creature] to the superior beauty of man" (158). As Mellor describes it, Frankenstein "is afraid of an independent female will, afraid that his female creature will have desires and opinions that cannot be controlled by his male creature" (119). The creature's nascent mate is thus the first female alien, and Frankenstein's revulsion for the creature marks the beginning of the tradition of woman-hating expressed through the horrific woman alien in mainstream science fiction. While there are other sources for science fiction's misogyny, the powerful threat posed by the female monster is a literal embodiment of the feminine qualities that shape all later female aliens: "For [Edmund] Burke, as for Victor Frankenstein, the most hideous monster of all is female " (Mellor 82). Yet it took Shelley's fiction to embody the female alien as so powerful that she could not even be allowed to breathe. Because of its influence, *Frankenstein*'s female monster can be seen as a harbinger of the misogynistic tradition that depicts and then destroys powerful female aliens. Shelley herself develops the woman alien in *The Last Man*, where the female alien destroys a civilization.

The Last Man, like *Frankenstein*, is marked by "structural indeterminacy" (Jackson 104). Both novels resist closure: traditional narrative structure, like the patriarchal symbolic order it evokes, is ruptured in the texts. Despite its very different critical reception, *The Last Man* is thematically similar to *Frankenstein*. Jackson emphasizes the importance of distinguishing between Shelley's authorial position, which invites criticism of the male societies she describes, and the male narrators' lament as patriarchy crumbles. Jackson reads the destruction of patriarchy in Shelley's novels as a "female gothic" because Shelley "fantasize[s] a violent attack upon the symbolic order" (103).

In science fiction, unlike the Gothic novel, a female writer can call upon a full panoply of destructive powers that cannot be combated by traditional patriarchal science. Through the failure of the traditional science it presents, feminist science fiction like *The Last Man* criticizes the scientific world, a world usually ignored by the Gothic novel. *The Last Man* reveals that "the domination of masculine values in the public realm can lead to the extinction of human life. . . . Only if they [men] too embrace a 'female consciousness,' will humanity survive" (Mellor 150–51). Shelley's novels produce not only a strain of the uncanny and inexplicable but also the explicable revolt of women who draw on an alternative science to destroy patriarchy. This tactic is first employed by Shelley, but later writers including Russ, Charnas, Butler, and McIntyre also use natural disasters to destroy the male symbolic order. Narrative structure and alternative science are related; the Gothic ethos combined with a critique of science produces a trenchant exposé of the problems of science.

The Last Man appears to be, like *Frankenstein*, a novel without important female characters, but reading the novel as codedly feminine reveals its feminist warning. Shelley uses apocalypse to expose humanity's vulnerability to Nature, a female destroyer. Nature is conventionally referred to as female, an oblique reference to Demeter, but Shelley stresses the female association by assigning femininity to the disease, which is referred to as PLAGUE and personified as female. PLAGUE is a version of Demeter, laying waste to the patriarchal world that has angered it. At first, war appears to be the great annihilator, but PLAGUE, a natural disease that only attacks humans, reveals the relative insignificance of *man*-made plague. Science is absolutely helpless against PLAGUE, which destroys without reference to rank. Before PLAGUE, England divests itself of the monarchy but retains other forms of aristocracy. PLAGUE makes nonsense of the king's abdication by showing how superfluous wealth and position are. The king's grand renunciation of his power proves meaningless, as do the wars and political conflicts that are described in some detail. The whole world is destroyed by PLAGUE and the activities of a male-dominated social order seem to be ridiculous posturings. The gendered nature of this position is emphasized when the women in the narrator's family wander away while the men remain "to discuss the affairs of nations, and the philosophy of life" (*Last Man* 65). England, a patriarchal culture—like all societies, even in Shelley's vision of the twenty-first century—is laid to waste by PLAGUE, the female destroyer that "had become Queen of the World" (252). By extrapolating the association of woman with Nature, Shelley can use a metaphor to represent feminine power. "In a patriarchal culture where women are identified with nature, with the object or the thing in itself, women writers are apt to blur the distinction between the literal and the figurative" (Mellor 163). As in *Frankenstein,* Shelley stresses female reproductive power in *The Last Man.* PLAGUE's most terrifying strength is its ability to regenerate each spring, after hibernating every winter. In its evocation of the first winter, PLAGUE is Demeter gone permanently mad. In Shelley's futuristic scenario, Nature destroys her children, just as Frankenstein attempts to murder his creature and destroys its female mate.

In a corresponding demonstration of the power of the feminine, Shelley's postapocalyptic setting provides Lionel Verney, last man and narrator, with an opportunity to demonstrate the transcendence of art over science.[8] Science and government alike are powerless, unable to stop PLAGUE, but as Lessing's representative for Planet 8 will do, Verney salvages part of his culture through art. His narrative not only preserves the past but also warns later civilizations. In *The Last Man,* Shelley provides another paradigm for feminist revisionists: the redemptive power of art reworked through the feminine. In this construction, art appears feminine because it is cast in the role of Other by science, which is resolutely masculine. In this reading, Verney functions as a stand-in for the feminist artist, as his identification with Sibyl suggests. The writing symbolizes art's power to preserve and bear witness because only Verney's narrative records the life and death of that human civilization. Even before the opening of the narrative, Shelley claims its author discovered the narrative in "Sibyl's cave" and that the writings were found on "Sibylline leaves" (3). Edith Hamilton describes Sybil as "a woman of deep wisdom, who could foretell the future," and whose story, hidden in "Sibyl's cave," exists as "Sibylline leaves" (226). Mellor argues that, through this reference, "Shelley thus invokes the ultimate female literary authority, the oracle of Sibyl, to authenticate her prophetic vision" (158).

Through Verney as Sibyl, Shelley points the way toward soft science, toward witchlike power, feminine power, rather than the science that provided machines "to supply with facility every want of the population" (*Last Man* 76). Ironically, the narrator's friend predicts that the Earth will become a Paradise, and the male futurist Merrival makes a similar prophecy. Men make the error of relying on science, but PLAGUE shows them the futility of such a dependence. As will happen in Lessing's Canopus in Argos series, art provides the only refuge when science fails. Through art, the patriarchal society can leave a warning to the future and a record of its past.

As its title implies, *The Last Man* also warns about the dangers of female exclusion. Like Walton, Verney suffers the pangs of great loneliness. His narrative graphically depicts his suffering as the sole survivor of a patriarchal culture, and he concludes ominously: "Beware tender offspring of the re-born world" (318). Shelley effectively uses the postapocalyptic setting as a Cassandra-like prophecy. If patriarchy insists on oppressing women and depending on male-dominated science, men will dwindle to the "last man."

The tremendous and continuing popularity of *Frankenstein* and the neglect of *The Last Man* after its initial popular reception require some explanation. What makes the former so acceptable and endlessly interpretable and the latter so unacceptable and rigid?[9] In each text Shelley adopts a different strategy of resistance. Her positions demonstrate two ways that feminist writers can proceed and the dangers inherent in each maneuver. These approaches can be usefully considered in the terms of deconstruction because the reactions to Shelley's texts provide an illustration of two strategies of resistance detailed by Jacques Derrida:

> a) To attempt the sortie and the deconstruction without changing ground, by repeating what is implicit in the founding concepts and original problematics, by using against the edifice the instruments or the stones available in the house, which means in language as well. The risk here is to constantly confirm, consolidate, or "relever," at a depth which is ever more sure, precisely that which we claim to be deconstructing. . . .
>
> b) to decide to change ground, in a discontinuous and eruptive manner, by stepping abruptly outside and by affirming absolute rupture and differ-

ence. . . . such a displacement (which dwells more naively than ever within
the inside that it claims to desert) . . . continually relocates the "new" ground
on the older one. (56)

Especially in its corrupted form, *Frankenstein* shows the dangers of deconstructing and yet replicating "what is implicit in the founding concepts."
Frankenstein is a radical and shocking novel, but whatever Shelley's political sympathies,[10] her text has been readily transformed into a conventional
horror story that reaffirms fears about the unknown and, for the first time,
about patriarchal science. *The Last Man,* in contrast, completely eradicates
traditional culture; the novel's setting steps "abruptly outside." According-
ly, *The Last Man* was ignored for over a century and its radical elements
were silenced. Neither strategy of resistance is completely successful.

What, then, are the lessons of Shelley's texts for later feminist writers?
Art provides a means of preservation, resistance, and salvation. In feminist
science fiction, art redeems women's culture, just as it preserves and criticizes Verney's patriarchal society in *The Last Man.* Lessing and other woman writers glorify art over science, as Shelley does. Feminist science fiction
takes Shelley's codedly female narrators and *Frankenstein'*s murdered female monster and gives them life. Through PLAGUE-like counterparts,
feminist science fiction exposes sexism and condemns female exclusion
from science and science fiction. Through the character of Frankenstein,
Shelley provides a voice for the female alien who never gets a chance to
speak, the mate for the monster. Pressured by the monster to create a female
monster, Frankenstein complies but cannot finish the project once he realizes the power a female monster would have.

As in many later works of science fiction, it is the female alien's ability to
reproduce that makes her so threatening to the male protagonist and patriarchal society. Frankenstein wrestles with his own potential fecundity throughout the book, affirming the depiction of woman as alien; it is his ability to
reproduce life scientifically that separates him from all other humans. The
isolation of the main characters from females emphasizes their fear of wom-
en: for all his vaunted love for Elizabeth, Frankenstein stays far away from
her; and although Walton writes longingly to his sister, his trip to the Arctic is
a self-imposed exile of years with only male companions. Like many works
of science fiction, *Frankenstein* is set in an all-male environment, a pattern
that persists even today in much science and science fiction.

Through the disastrous failure of Frankenstein's and Walton's scientific
explorations, Shelley shows that she was centuries ahead of her time, for

Frankenstein can be read as a warning about the dangers of female exclusion from science as well as about the powers of reproduction. The novel exposes Frankenstein and Walton for the failures of their male-dominated scientific inquiries: Frankenstein learns to his chagrin the cost of working alone and of keeping Elizabeth in ignorance, and Walton regrets the absence of his sister and forsakes his quest to reach the North Pole. In this way, the novel can be read as a fictional version of the theoretical work being done on gender and science that stresses the effect of gender on science—such as Keller's *Reflections on Gender and Science* and Haraway's *Primate Visions*. Later writers continue Shelley's emphasis on gender and science. For example, in Russ's "When It Changed," a disease has killed all the male settlers on a planet, but through their ability to merge ova, the female colonists survive, reproduce, and form a utopian society, if only for a while. Because, like Frankenstein, the female colonists have learned an alternative form of reproduction, they are female aliens. Like the female monster, they present the threat of women surviving and peopling a whole planet without men.

Russ's story, like *The Last Man* and numerous science fiction works by women, presents men as unable to survive an attack by nature, through a disease. In feminist science fiction, from nineteenth-century utopias to twentieth-century dystopias, the universe is reevaluated from the viewpoint of the female alien. Frankenstein's story is retold, not by another male explorer, but by female aliens in the guises of characters like the Mizorans in Lane's utopia or Moon in Vinge's *Snow Queen*. In contemporary science fiction by women, including Atwood's *Handmaid's Tale* and Lessing's *Shikasta*, the apocalyptic setting of *The Last Man* reappears transfigured as a feminist message—a warning about the dangers of male hubris. Before feminists realized her legacy, however, Shelley's message lay dormant in male science fiction for almost a century.

In a number of dystopias, Victorian novelists depict worlds in which the female monster comes to life and rules entire civilizations. These fictions draw on figures of woman that are double-edged; the witch, the Sphinx, and the Medusa are evoked again and again. One of the reasons these figures recur so frequently was the obsessive concern about women's roles in nineteenth-century culture, which, as Auerbach and Dijkstra demonstrate, manifests itself through the literature and painting of the period. As a part of this culture, science fiction continues this obsession, but the genre of science fiction provides a sharper delineation of these concerns because they are highlighted by science. Studying nineteenth-century science fiction reveals a heightened anxiety about women and science and exposes what nineteenth-century writers thought were the sources of female power: reproduction and alternative social structures based on models of mothering.

Appropriately for a genre that has been called the mythology of the modern world, science fiction rediscovers and revises older myths of female monsters like that of the Sphinx, who poses riddles and devours men for failing to answer correctly.[11] The Medusa is a similarly destructive female figure who appears frequently in science fiction and who, like the Sphinx, is associated with death. The Medusa is one of the three Gorgons, "'each with wings / And snaky hair, most horrible to mortals. Whom no man shall behold and draw again / the breath of life'"(Hamilton 143). Like the Sphinx, the Medusa is a hybrid, a mixture of animal and humanoid—and immortal. This association of woman with beast was commonplace, of course, in Victorian science; Darwin, among others, placed woman below man and closer on the evolutionary scale to the animals. What happens with the Medusa and female aliens in science fiction is that this association, viewed as a liability in the dominant culture, becomes a source of strength and power. It is her snaky hair that mesmerizes and paralyzes the man unhappy enough to view the Medusa.[12]

The witch, a third figure who shapes the depictions of female aliens, is primarily a Christian figure, although there are classical models for her, such as Medea. As "a female magician, sorceress" (*OED* 3798), the witch encompasses the Sphinx and the Medusa; and, indeed, in descriptions of female aliens, all three figures often are conflated. While the Sphinx and the Medusa are part animal, the witch is completely human (insomuch as any woman, in this context, is considered human). Woman's reproductive power alone made her "a mysterious being who communicates with spirits and thus has magic powers she can use to hurt the male'" (Karen Horney, qtd. in Rich 103). All three figures codified the sexual allure and paralyzing power that women could wield over men. The idea behind all three is that somehow a woman could mesmerize a man, compel him against his will. The Sphinx, the Medusa, and the witch represent woman as unknowable, uncontrollable, with unexplainable powers. They represent nature, and against nature, especially in the nineteenth century, man wielded the tool of science.

Repeatedly in science fiction written by men, a male explorer or scientist confronts female aliens who evoke specters of female power and confound them through science. It is by encountering the female alien that the male hero (and presumably the male reader of the text) recognizes and defines his own masculinity and that of the dominant culture. The idea of hard and soft science fiction also applies to science—the hard science of the male protagonist is challenged by the soft science of the Sphinx, the Medusa, and the witch. The ultimate softness lies in the womb, in the female power as mother to swathe the male child both before and after birth. The psychoanalytic dynamic described by Nancy Chodorow in which the male child must repudiate his mother to assert his masculinity (176) underlies the appearances of the Sphinx, the Medusa, and the witch in science fiction. Only in science fiction can this psychoanalytic pattern be metaphorically dramatized. Womblike worlds with female aliens appear frequently, as, for example, in the underground world in Bulwer-Lytton's *Coming Race*. Such worlds are an extrapolation of the female power to reproduce that appears first in Shelley's *Frankenstein*.

The female alien frequently appears as part of an entire society, the female dystopia, or an apocalyptic and regressive society run by women, or an all-female world. The female dystopia is usually populated by female aliens, but a female dystopia is more apocalyptic than most fictions about societies of aliens, for men have been completely overruled by women or, in some cases, have completely disappeared. These settings have been neglected by science fiction critics for two reasons. First, most dystopias do not live up to the imaginative and stylistic standards of the genre; they are thinly disguised attacks on women, and their authors pay little attention to extrapolation, plot, or writing. Second, the misogyny of these texts is so virulent that even a critic indifferent to feminism would find it difficult to ignore. However, the female dystopias were often immensely popular, and for this reason alone more attention must be paid to this tradition, which still flourishes. The female dystopia contains the elements that most uninformed readers envision when they think of science fiction: scantily clad females attacked by monsters and rescued by men. The misogyny of the female dystopia explains why some critics are surprised by woman science fiction writers, but, as will be made clear, the female dystopia must be seen as the progenitor of feminist science fiction.

Previous interpretations of female dystopias, such as Russ's "*Amor Vincit Foeminam:* The Battle of the Sexes in Science Fiction," describe the role reversals and literal wars between the sexes (2). Russ discusses female dystopias as the natural concomitant to female utopias. However, these two types are not only parallel, they also intersect. Female dystopias need to be read historically as precursors as well as companions to the female utopias discussed in chapter 3. They must be read in conjunction with an analysis of the female alien, who is, after all, both citizen and ruler of the female dystopia. While Russ appropriately criticizes the inept writing and logical fallacies of these texts, she neglects the connection between the particular way that women are portrayed in these worlds and in science fiction tradition. For example, in her discussion of Parley Cooper's misogynistic depiction of a world run by women, entitled *The Feminists,*[13] Russ stresses the incoherence of the plot. But in that novel, along with its individual difficulties as narrative, there is the coherence of allusions to *Frankenstein* and reproduction, allusions that reveal the pattern to female dystopias that can be traced back to Shelley.

The woman ruler of a dystopia ironically asserts female subordination by first supplying women with social, economic, and political dominance. This dystopian pattern sets up female rule only to show how women would abuse such power. In female dystopias, the theme of the evil and incompetent woman ruler dominates; the pattern recurs over a hundred years and provides mainstream science fiction writers with a ready-made, negative depiction of women in the future.

The Coming Race by Bulwer-Lytton is the first important dystopia of female aliens. This popular novel influenced Wells's science fiction and, through Wells, the rest of the male science fiction tradition.[14] The plot of *The Coming Race* prepares the reader for Wells's *Time Machine* and later female dystopias. Bulwer-Lytton's hero is a male explorer who inadvertently discovers an alien race living in the bowels of the Earth. By his mere presence, the human hero throws the alien society into chaos. However, instead of dominating the alien society, the explorer finds himself being dominated by the race's females—an uncomfortable position for a Victorian gentleman. He discovers that the Vril-ya, the aliens, are a female-dominated society ruled on the basis of superior powers that are connected to the powers of human women (such as the power to give birth or the magical powers associated with witches). The aliens' mental powers make them a formidable species, and the narrator eventually escapes from the Vril-ya to warn humans of the Coming Race.

The novel's conclusion reveals how ominous its title is. The aliens have a legend that explains how the Vril-ya were sent to live in the bowels of the Earth to perfect themselves, and when their development is completed, they will return to the surface. With their superior physique (they are long-lived) and their skill in psionics, these aliens could quickly dominate the human race. Most frightening to the Victorian hero is the fact that the Vril-ya appear to have evolved faster than humans. The alien females in particular terrify the narrator; their domination of him makes the Vril-ya's domination of humanity seem inevitable.

In Bulwer-Lytton's novel, as in many works of science fiction, female characters are depicted as especially alien because of their sex. Although both sexes of the Vril-ya are literally alien to the narrator, the females of the race are even more distinctly other than the males: the females "were of taller stature and ampler proportions than the males; and their countenances, if still more symmetrical in outline and contour, were devoid of the softness and timidity of expression which gave charm to the face of woman as seen in the earth above" (262). The Vril-ya believe that women are supposed to be stronger and larger than men and refer the human narrator to the insect world for evidence. The Vril-ya belief in female superiority and the evidence of their females reflect ironically on the narrator's assumption of male primacy in the human race. Male dominance, Bulwer-Lytton implies, may rely more on custom than on nature. By their existence, these female aliens throw doubt on the security of patriarchy.

The physical description of the Gy-ei (the name for the females of the Vril-ya who dominate the world inside the Earth) emphasizes the symbolic connection of the female aliens with human women. The narrator notices that the Gy-ei have faces like the Sphinx—female, inscrutable, and powerful. Like the Sphinx, the Gy-ei loom over the narrator; he is dwarfed by their size and the powers of their witchlike alternative science. Significantly, the narrator also compares the Gy-ei to witches: "I felt a terror and the wild excitement with which, in the Gothic ages, a traveller might have persuaded himself that he witnessed a *sabbat* of fiends and witches" (265). Like many other science fiction writers, Bulwer-Lytton conflates the figures of the Sphinx and the witch and draws on the historical association of men with science and women with magic to make his aliens terrifying. Like woman healers and midwives, the Gy-ei threaten male dominance and control. Writers of female dystopias justify witch-burning and advocate the suppression of all women, lest powerful females threaten patriarchy.

Although historically witches and magic were suppressed by patriarchy, Bulwer-Lytton presents alternative science as a still powerful and frightening force. He connects magic with reproduction, a conjunction that presents the possibility of the Gy-ei overwhelming man through intermarriage. Through their power as mothers, the female aliens could slowly destroy mankind by diluting its bloodlines. The apparently magical quality of their technology is presented as evil and dangerous. The connection of Gy-ei alternative science with witches is negative; through that analogy, Bulwer-Lytton affirms the strangeness and dangerousness of woman. The superior power of the Vril-ya implicitly rests "on their supposedly stronger sexual energy" (Suvin, *Metamorphoses* 347). As a final and, to the modern reader, humorous confirmation of the Gy-ei usurpation of the male role, while the males are beardless, the Gy-ei sprout mustaches in their old age.

Although Bulwer-Lytton never mentions the New Woman on the surface of the Earth, his female aliens are clearly related to human women. Although his novel appears less antifemale than a novel like Besant's *Revolt of Man,* which contains human women rather than aliens, his message is dystopian. The Gy-ei show what emancipated human females could become; the sub-ordinated alien males and the frightened narrator show how helpless men could be. The alienness of the Vril-ya reveals how masculine power might change women and how powerful women can destroy patriarchal culture. Bulwer-Lytton uses science fiction to warn that men may find themselves superseded if they fail to use science to keep woman in a subordinate posi-tion. Metaphorically, the Coming Race refers to the New Woman.

Although the extent of female power in Vril-ya society frightens the nar-rator, he is reassured to notice that the alien "females are in practice prevent-ed from using their superiority" (Suvin, *Metamorphoses* 347). This is the same pattern Auerbach identifies in Victorian fantasy, where only "at the last minute [is the mythic female figure] prevented from extending her reign beyond the looking-glass into the reader's reality" (*Demon* 36). In the fe-male dystopia, a horrific world to the beleaguered male narrator, the threat of female dominance justifies suppressing women. Bulwer-Lytton's novel recommends oppressing females and developing science so as to be able to defeat the formidable Coming Race, which is depicted in an unabashedly negative way. For example, the location of the Vril-ya world in the bowels of the Earth evokes Hell and emphasizes Bulwer-Lytton's many references to witches, who are associated with the devil. The writers who follow Bul-wer-Lytton are less blunt, but the tradition continues of presenting woman as a dangerous species distinct from man. Bulwer-Lytton's paradigm set the pattern for the tradition of woman as alien and woman as potential ruler of mankind.

In female dystopias, the female ruler inevitably and eagerly forsakes her power, as the novel that crystallizes this tradition shows. Besant's *Revolt of Man,* published in 1882, is a role-reversal dystopia set in 2082. A primer of the evils caused by female rulers, it demonstrates a fanatical fear of female education and the suffragists. Besant's future females not only give up their authority but conclude that female subordination is natural (Russ, *Amor* 3). At the end of the novel, all women are legally confined to their homes in a mass house-arrest. Although Besant's female characters are not literally aliens, they are treated as such.

The confinement of women in *The Revolt of Man* is presented as natural and appropriate. In female dystopias, women reign because physical force has been sublimated. What is referred to as the Great Transition in Besant's book occurred because men would not use their brute strength. Male chivalry, the author claims, led to the worship of the Perfect Woman and men therefore abdicated their claim to authority. According to Besant, women enjoy indolence at the expense of men so that both sexes behave like animals rather than civilized beings. "In animal creation, again, it is the male who works, while the female sits and directs" (124), explains one of the characters, a professor of natural history. At first the natural world is cited to justify female dominance, but by the conclusion, Besant shows the reader that women have misunderstood natural history. The stagnant culture demonstrates that women rulers would artificially end human progress.

In this type of dystopia, female rulers are inevitably incompetent and the list of ills the all-female rule causes is endless. The Royal Academy Show of Art consists of nothing but heroic representations of women: Jael, Joan of Arc, and the Perfect Woman. "Of course, all the artists were women" (105)—and "of course" this leads to the stagnation of art. Year after year the subjects are the same and all the pictures painted are exactly alike. Literature, especially the novel, also suffers. Smollett, Dickens, and even Shakespeare are banned because of their antifemale slant. University education has also been bowdlerized by women. Christianity is abandoned and instead religion focuses on the worship of the Perfect Woman. The domination of women continues through matrilineage and a powerful female aristocracy.

Most significant of the ills caused by female rule is the neglect of science. In *The Revolt of Man,* technological advances cease and old achievements are abandoned. As the history professor, a traitor to her sex, explains: "We took from men their education and science was forgotten" (142). The railroads are gone, and Manchester has become a bucolic backwater. Women have taken England from factories back to the spinning wheel. This revolution occurred not by choice but because women "cannot create; because at no time has any woman enriched the world with a new idea, a new truth, a new discovery, a new invention" (143). This virulent speech from the history professor explains why women should not be allowed to control anything, let alone a country. Even this highly educated and politically powerful woman has only learned the failings of her sex. Besant warns that if women are allowed rights, scientific advances will be lost. The irreconcilability of woman and science is the main lesson of *The Revolt of Man.*

Besant's novel shows that in an all-female-ruled world, the educated woman embodies evil. Women rulers would be godless, scienceless, and sexually aggressive. Because of women's incapacity, men deserve to rule the world. That this state of affairs has divine blessing is emphasized by Christianity's role in the men's revolt. Only men can be true Christians, because woman intrinsically desire to be worshiped themselves. The bishop's daughter, Grace, the new Perfect Woman, explains, "Happy the women of old, when there was no woman employed, and each was the goddess of one man" (221). In the end, a utopia of female subordination is achieved and the dystopia of female rule abolished. In a world run by women, the human race degenerates as scientific advancement ceases. The loss of technology provides the surest sign of female incapacity and the strongest justification for female subordination. Besant extols science as the male religion based on natural female inferiority. His message is the irreconcilability of woman and science. Men deserve to rule women because only the masculine command of science improves the culture.

The association of the female alien with female incapacity for science appears prominently in Wells's *Time Machine*. Ironically, Wells was, in other contexts, an advocate of feminism. Although he could expose oppression up to a point in a realistic novel like *Anne Veronica,* his science fiction, perhaps because of the genre's history, reveals a fundamental distrust of women and suggests an ambivalence about women's equality. Wells appears to have wanted women to have the traditionally masculine quality of rationality, because in his science fiction, femininity is depicted as dangerously weakening. Besant's influence on Wells is most evident in *The Time Machine*,[15] which, like *The Revolt of Man,* is about effeminate evolution: both writers depict a future world based on feminine values, worlds in which scientific progress has ceased. In Wells's Earth of 802,702, one branch of humanity shares "the same soft hairless visage, and the same girlish rotundity of limb" (22). Feminism is the cause of this feminization of the human form. The sexes have become less specialized and their bodies have adapted to sexual equality. "The specialization of the sexes with reference to their children's needs disappears. . . . We see some beginnings of this even in our own time" (22), the narrator theorizes.

Rather than an androgynous synthesis,[16] however, the Eloi act out the stereotypical feminine role. They are passive, childlike in intellect, and devoted to adornment. Peter Nicholls describes them as appearing "feminine, beautiful, carefree and irresponsible" and explains that "a magazine illustration by Virgil Finlay makes the point clear" (Nicholls 537). Again and again, the Time Traveller compares the Eloi to women. They react like a "delicate-minded woman" (28) and have "the softness of a woman" (22).

Wells underscores their femininity through his description of the Time Traveller's constant companion, Weena, who represents all the Eloi. The Time Traveller functions as the male scientists/saviors do in the female dystopias; like them, he rescues an individual and then receives her complete devotion. Weena and her species are the degenerate females seen in *The Revolt of Man, Virgin Planet,* and so many other female dystopias; the Time Traveller is the explorer who destroys the all-female world by his presence.

Like the female dystopias, the Eloi world is handicapped by the complete atrophy of science. Wells's portrait of the Eloi implies the deadly consequences of sexual equality for human evolution. The Eloi's closeness to nature echoes the female dystopias' emphasis on woman-nature; similarly, in science fiction a "natural" culture is a degenerate and weak one. "The softness of a woman" (22) means the women have no weapons and are incapable of defending themselves. The Eloi will not fight; they are the antithesis of the narrator, a hardy male explorer. In fact, the Eloi are prey for the brutal race that lives underground—the Morlocks.

The identification of the Eloi as a feminine race is underscored by the White Sphinx. The Sphinx posed the riddle to Oedipus, as the Eloi do to the Time Traveller. John Huntington suggests the Sphinx's significance as the representative of an achievement that is actually a regression, the degeneration of human civilization (44). The decadence of the Eloi replicates the degeneration and passivity of the cultures of female dystopias. Again, an illustration by Finlay supports this interpretation of *The Time Machine* as a female dystopia. His Sphinx crystallizes the depiction of the evil female ruler as she looms threateningly like the immobile wombs of Farmer's "Mother."

While the Eloi represent femininity, the Morlocks represent masculinity. This dichotomy parallels the most commonly discussed interpretation of *The Time Machine,* that of workers versus owners. As Nicholls explains, "the two races allegorize 19th-century sexual distinctions and class distinctions simultaneously" (537). The Time Traveller's vehement hatred of the Morlocks suggests that he has more in common with them than he is willing to admit. He concedes that he has no scientific reason to hate the Morlocks and that he sides with the Eloi because of their superficial appearance. Like him, the Morlocks are fierce, warlike, and more intelligent and curious than the Eloi. The Morlocks oil, clean, and dismantle the narrator's Time Machine, and the hum of machinery dominates their underground abode. While the Eloi have degenerated to an animalistic dependence on nature, the Morlocks live in an artificial environment, again more like hu-

"And now I was to see the most weird and horrible scene of all that I had beheld in that future age."

11

THE TIME MACHINE

Defenseless, alone, he blazed his nightmare trail into Tomorrow, the grim Traveler who dared to gamble the world—to live again a million years too late!

CHAPTER I

THE INVENTOR

THE man who made the Time Machine—the man I shall call The Time Traveler—was well known in scientific circles a few years since, and the fact of his disappearance is also well known. He was a mathematician of peculiar subtlety and one of our most conspicuous investigators in molecular physics. He did not confine himself to abstract science. Several inventions, and one or two very profitable patents were his; able they were, these but, as his handsome house at Richmond testifies. To those who were his intimates, however, his scientific investigations were as nothing to his gift of speech.

In the after-dinner hours he was ever a vivid and variegated talker, and at times his fantastic, often paradoxical, conceptions came so thick and close as to form one continuous discourse. At these times he was as unlike the popular conceptions of a scientific investigator as a man could be. His cheeks would flush, his eyes grow bright, and the stranger the

By
H. G.
Wells

10

Above me towered the sphinx . . . white, shin-
ing, leprous in the light of the rising moon.

25

mans. They have not forgotten science, as is demonstrated by their underground cities and their intricate metalwork. Their bestial appearance and cannibalism are merely the Time Traveller's own characteristics magnified. He delights in killing the Morlocks, and his first action on returning is to demand meat: "I'm starving for a bit of meat. . . . What a treat it is to stick a fork into meat again" (11–12). Not for him the frugivorous diet of the Eloi. In his discussion of Wells's later novels, Peter Kemp stresses that "meat-cravings and masculinity are closely associated in Wells's mind" (47). Kemp also notes the recurring paradigm of the female object being pursued by the amorous male predator, a pattern that fits *The Time Machine* as well.

In part because he is like them, the narrator turns from the Morlocks in revulsion. While the Eloi inspire protective feelings in the Time Traveller, the Morlocks produce feelings of competition and hate. The narrator returns to the future to battle the Morelocks for the possession of the world and of the Eloi, further emphasizing the male-Morlock identification: it is the primitive battle of men over women. The novel's silence about the outcome of the Time Traveller's second trip points to the dangers for the narrator as well as for the human race of following the path to androgyny. The Time Traveller never returns from that trip, and the novel closes with "two strange white flowers—shrivelled now, and brown and flat and brittle" (66). These are the flowers that Weena, the Time Traveller's female Eloi companion, gave to him, as dead as she and the Time Traveller presumably are.

Again, Wells's debt to Besant is striking: in a sermon in *The Revolt of Man,* the preacher emphasizes that man has always served woman (123)—and man's service to womanhood results in the unnatural domination of woman rulers. Similarly, the Time Traveller theorizes that the Morlocks had been the Eloi's servants. Like the English women in *The Revolt of Man,* who find themselves prisoners of the men, the Eloi suffer the horrible consequences of their oppression of the Morlocks. The danger, then, in female emancipation is that hyperfemininity produces hypermasculinity. Through the evolution of humanity into Eloi and Morlocks, Wells stresses the evolutionary dangers of female equality. His portrait of the Eloi is strikingly similar to Besant's depiction of women in *The Revolt of Man* or to the women in Poul Anderson's much later *Virgin Planet.* The moral is the same: a female culture means cultural degeneration.

At the same time, Wells points to hard science as salvation. Women and science are irreconcilable, as Weena's fear of matches and the Eloi's neglect of the museum of natural history show. Again, the male scientist-explorer is the hero. His chivalry, bravery, attractiveness to women, and, most important, his scientific knowledge make him putative master of this future Earth. This paradigm is precisely the pattern of *The Revolt of Man* and other female dystopias. *The Time Machine* reveals how the male science fiction tradition builds on the female dystopia. Even Wells, the writer who has been described as the "founding father of science fiction" (Conklin vii), imagines aliens through the female dystopian lens.

The journey from Shelley to Wells takes less than one hundred years, but those are important decades for science and, concomitantly, for science fiction. The impact of Shelley's encoding feminist concerns into what has been acclaimed by many as the first modern novel of science fiction continues to make its influence felt into the 1990s. But the course of the channel changes. Some writers, particularly feminist science fiction writers, draw directly on Shelley's text; others, especially male writers, take their inspiration from Wells and do not realize the way in which his aliens were affected by hers. What *Frankenstein, The Last Man, The Coming Race, The Revolt of Man,* and *The Time Machine* demonstrate is that gender is inextricably connected to questions of science, and the ways writers conceptualize science is shaped by their attitudes toward reproduction. These texts reveal that gender defines the evaluation and appreciation of science, at least in fictional depictions, and that science is an important site of legitimation. They suggest that science can be used to determine social power and help to explain why male characters and male writers so vehemently deny science to female characters and writers, and why feminist writers from Shelley to Lessing feel compelled to write science fiction.

Notes

1. Many critics have complained about science fiction's misogyny. For early feminist critiques of science fiction see Friend, "Virgin Territory"; Le Guin, "American SF and the Other"; Badami, "A Feminist Critique of Science Fiction"; and Monk, "Frankenstein's Daughters." Unfortunately, most of their criticisms are still applicable.

2. As Chris Baldick points out, "Modern criticism has been able to read *Frankenstein* in a number of ways which go well beyond the formerly accepted interpretation of the novel as simple cautionary tale; in so many ways, indeed, that the variety becomes bewildering" (55).

3. I agree with William Veeder that "a critic [of *Frankenstein*] today must seek not the false stability of any totalizing explanation but the legitimate coherence of a

reading consistent with itself, a reading which consciously recognizes its partial quality as it follows a single thread or threads through the whole fabric" (89).

4. See Charles Platt's profile of James Tiptree, Jr. (Alice Sheldon), for a discussion of her use of codedly female narrators (257–72). Catherine Podojil identifies a related phenomenon in "Sisters, Daughters, and Aliens" and explains that "women writers in the field of science fiction have often found themselves adopting traditionally male techniques or points of view. Some writers have changed or disguised their names" (70–71).

5. Robin Morgan explains that "women develop the skill of such translation (for Algerian read female—because the author assuredly will not extend his insights in your direction)" (231).

6. This myth is one that Shelley used explicitly in a play, *Prosperine,* where the goddess Ceres vows to make the earth barren (Veeder 167), but there are many implicit allusions to this myth about mothering in her other fictions.

7. Sandra Gilbert and Susan Gubar also assert the centrality of "disguised, buried, or miniaturized, femaleness . . . at the heart of this apparently masculine book" (232). The novel has even been read by Barbara Johnson "as the autobiography of a woman" (57).

8. Verney may be associated with "vernal" and Shelley may be indirectly referring to the Demeter myth through his name. I am indebted to Wendy Flory for this suggestion.

9. Hugh Lake, the modern editor of *The Last Man,* recounts: "*The Last Man* had little popular success and was damned by critics" (viii).

10. Paul O'Flinn suggests that Shelley's radical politics are an integral part of her text, and he cites her letters and the book's dedication to show her sympathy for radical political causes. He also details the ways in which *Frankenstein* was co-opted, especially in the film versions.

11. According to *The Oxford Classical Dictionary,* the Sphinx was "first adopted by Greek artists as a type of ghost-like monsters who carry off boys or youths and are present at fatal combat. . . . [The Sphinx] was placed on tombs" (2d ed., 1009). This image of the predatory women carrying off young males suggests that nineteenth-century male fears have a venerable source in the ancient world. Her presence on tombs emphasizes the association of the Sphinx with death. The feminine essence of the Sphinx is underscored by the fact that, in the later versions of the myth, she is sent to Thebes by Hera, vengeful and jealous wife and sister of Zeus. There the Sphinx poses her riddle of the three ages of man and carries away and eats those who fail to solve the riddle.

The riddle's emphasis on the development of individuals, the Sphinx's insistence that ontogeny recapitulates phylogeny, would suggest evolution to late nineteenth-century readers, as it does to filmmaker Laura Mulvey, who says: "I think of the Sphinx as standing for the danger, the threat posed by femininity in patriarchal society, which is closely linked to motherhood." Mulvey explains that the Sphinx stands "for that which is in or of femininity which cannot be described/understood by a society that assigns the feminine inferior value" (qtd. in Suter and Flitterman 95). Failure to solve the riddle of evolution could result in death. The riddle casts woman in opposition to man and man as both the subject of the riddle and its object. Man is cast in the role of victim, of a meal for the superior organism, the Sphinx. The legend even ends equivocally; the Sphinx either commits suicide or is killed by Oedipus, who, of course, meets his own doom in the figure of his mother. In either case, the Sphinx is vanquished.

12. Her abode also draws on the fear of the unknown, which is central to science fiction: to find the Medusa, Perseus must have the help of the Gray Women. The gorgons live in a remote and inaccessible area, a setting like that of alien worlds. With gifts from Athena that evoke technology—winged sandals, a mirrored shield, and a cap that made him invisible—Perseus is able to behead the Medusa. Again, the use of tools to defeat and control women is central to science fiction's female aliens. Significantly, it is to female powers that Perseus turns; only other females are able to help him locate and then defeat the Medusa.

13. The jacket copy for Cooper's book reads in part: "They rule the world, and the top dog is a bitch. . . . 1992: To Be a Man is a Sin."

14. See Bergonzi (43) and Philmus (17–19). In his autobiography, Wells recalls that in the 1890s he "was welcomed as . . . a second Bulwer Lytton" (qtd. in Parrinder, *Wells* 77).

15. A contemporary reviewer, Israel Zangwill, in the column "Without Prejudice" in *Pall Mall* (September 1895, vii, 153–55), notes the similarity in theme between Wells's *Time Machine* and Besant's *Inner House* (qtd. in Parrinder, *Wells* 40).

16. Carolyn Heilbrun explains: "This ancient Greek word—from *andro* (male) and *gyn* (female)—defines a condition under which the characteristics of the sexes, and the human impulses expressed by men and women, are not rigidly assigned" (*Recognition* x).

TWO

The Female Alien: Pulp Science Fiction's Legacy to Feminists

T hough science fiction itself at first seems an inhospitable place for feminist ideas, the patterns of science fiction provide women writers with the opportunity for radical revision and reclamation. Nina Auerbach, demonstrating the workings of such symbolic revamping in Victorian culture, writes that "Woman [is] enlarged by myth" (*Demon* 15), even by myths that demonize females; in science fiction, woman is literally enlarged. Because of the depiction of femininity as magical, reproductive, dangerous, and threatening to men, female monsters, literal aliens, and female rulers all belong in the category of female alien. The obsession with Woman that is present mythically, but diffusely, in Victorian science fiction becomes a central focus in twentieth-century science fiction. The chapters that follow focus on analyses of female utopias and feminist science fiction, but this chapter presents a parallel history of male writers and artists who sustained the depiction of women as powerful. It is placed here because the pulp science fiction magazines were read and absorbed by the contemporary women writers who are discussed later.

Images of powerful women embodied in the figure of the female alien and the woman ruler in nineteenth-century fiction are expanded and depicted most graphically in the American tradition of "pulp" magazines (so called because of the cheap, pulpy paper on which they were printed). These magazines provide the clearest images of women's strength, and they are also worth studying because of their connection with contemporary science fiction. For many of today's science fiction writers, the golden era of science fiction was the 1940s and 1950s, when pulp magazines flourished. These magazines provided and encouraged a fan-writer-editor interaction that promulgated a sense of belonging to an elite subculture.[1] Many well known and popular science fiction writers, including Isaac Asimov and Robert Heinlein, received their start in the pulp science fiction magazines, and many prominent feminist writers were introduced to the genre through the pulps. Despite the influential role of pulp magazines, most critics of science fiction have neglected them, perhaps understandably, for the magazines are ephemeral and rarely represented in academic libraries. Despite their neglect in the academic world, pulp magazines deserve our attention because they were popular, influential, and their patterns help explain the emergence of feminist science fiction.

A reader perusing one of the few books containing reprints from the pulp science fiction magazines might think that such publications would be the last place feminist writers would find inspiration. The covers and stories represented in books like James Gunn's *Alternate Worlds* typically display the clichéd image of an enormous, bizarre-looking, and malignant alien carrying away a curvaceous woman. This stereotypical view of science fiction is belied, however, by the issues raised by the depiction of woman in these magazines. While the stories are formulaic, the interaction between the cover art and cover stories in pulp science fiction magazines demonstrates that the female alien and the woman ruler were transformed in a way that rendered them available for feminist appropriation. The scantily clad cover girls undoubtedly attracted attention and sold copies, but they also emphasize the feminine and evoke the maternal: the female aliens are frequently gigantic and loom over the men, and the emphasis on their immense, engorged breasts evokes the image of mother. Nearly naked women emphasize the biological differences between male and female, differences that have led critics like Sam Moskowitz to declare, "The implication [in science fiction] is almost that a male and female are two completely different species" (*Strange* 90). This depiction is often represented as literally true in science fiction novels, as, for example, in Larry Niven's *Ringworld,* where the narrator counts male and female as distinct species. In pulp science fiction, the most dangerous alien is the female alien who can mesmerize men through sexual allure or reproduce and overwhelm humankind. Of course, sexuality and reproduction are related psychoanalytically, visually, and through the plot of the stories, in which the men are dependent on the female alien for life itself.

Edward G. Bulwer-Lytton and his contemporaries H. Rider Haggard and Edwin Abbott kept this misogynistic legacy alive in the Victorian era. In *The Coming Race,* Bulwer-Lytton depicts a race dominated by its women; the narrator himself is threatened by a female alien who wants to marry him. Similarly, Haggard's *She* (1887), while not, strictly speaking, science fiction, crystallizes the powerful and sexually alluring female alien through Ayesha, the "she" of the title, who rules over a race and is revered as a goddess.[2] In Abbott's classic *Flatland* (1884), "a Female . . . is a creature by no means to be trifled with" (12). While not sexually attractive to the human eye, women in Flatland possess great powers. Because they are straight lines (all beings in Flatland are geometric shapes), they can make themselves invisible and their points are deadly: "The whole male population of a village has been sometimes destroyed in one or two hours of simultaneous female outbreak" (14).[3] The paradigm of the large, powerful female alien dominates the depiction of women in the pulps, especially in the late forties and fifties, when science fiction magazines experienced a great boom.[4]

The "big boom" in pulp magazines occurred at the same time as another boom—the baby boom. The primacy of the mother in the nuclear family and the widening acceptance of Freudian psychology meant that no one questioned "the race of the educated American woman back to the home" (Friedan 114). The sudden reemergence of female aliens in the science fiction pulps during this time may well have been a by-product of the post–World War II glorification of femininity. The exodus of woman from the factories[5] reflects a dual anxiety about "unnatural" women like Bulwer-Lytton's formidable female aliens, who dominate the public world, and the psychological power women could wield as rulers of the domestic sphere, as the "Angels of the House." Pulp science fiction, however, more quickly reflected the anxiety this massive cultural shift caused. In these texts, female aliens who are rulers and superior to men—politically, scientifically, or both—renounce their achievements and defer to human males, sometimes at the cost of their lives. Because of their maternal qualities, woman's self-abnegation is presented as admirable. These stories describe a patriarchal symbolic order in which the maternal is expected to destroy itself to preserve the patriarchy.

The depiction of gigantic female aliens dominating a human male suggests a psychoanalytic interpretation, but the mother/son conflict is often presented overtly. For example, in Philip José Farmer's "Mother" (1953), the female alien is a giant womb for a human male who stimulates her reproductive processes and then regresses to a fetal stage. Farmer's outrageously blatant version of the Mother as both sexual object and nurturer exposes the virulence of misogyny and its intense anxiety about any version of female power. Through its condemnation of the Mother alien for engorging the human male, Farmer's story nauseatingly illustrates the obsession

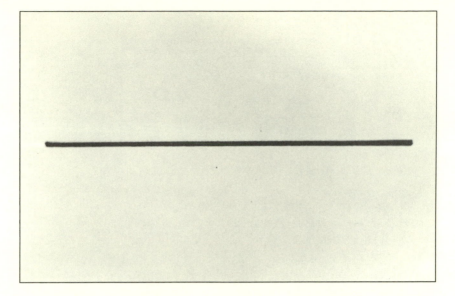

with the mother that feminist critics like Julia Kristeva discuss. Role reversals in pulp science fiction depict this anxiety in bizarre and unusual characterizations that deserve investigation.

Pulp science fiction cover art emphasizes the female alien's strengths, particularly her physical prowess and sexual allure. It also stresses the natural or supernatural source of female strength. Nature is depicted as feminine, while the male characters depend exclusively on technology. For example, a *Planet Stories* cover by Vestal Wood depicts a fully outfitted and armed astronaut overwhelmed by three bathing beauties. In pulp magazines, the nature/science dichotomy becomes a female/male split, a split mirrored in the larger culture. What appears as a strength in the illustrations develops into a handicap in the texts: Farmer's female aliens are killed by their own reproductive cycle; a witch is destroyed by her own sexual desires; a gigantic mermaid is killed by her emergence into the world of men. In each case, physically and mentally inferior men bring about the death of the most formidable female aliens. At the same time, these writers and artists evoke legendary women of power— mermaids, lamia, the Medusa, the demonic women that fascinated Victorian culture (Auerbach, *Demon* 8–9). Science fiction gave this Victorian paradigm of demonic woman new life; she was kept alive but enslaved, carefully circumscribed in text, though not in illustrations.

Because the illustrations emphasize the beginnings of the pulp stories in

which the female aliens are still powerful, the pictures provide a visual image of feminine strength that the stories defeat. This tension explains why both male and female readers could enjoy the pulp magazines. The influence of such publications is described by Andrea Lorraine Fuller, who told me: "I've been reading science fiction since the mid-1940s. I read the stories for the beginnings—men may have been reading for the endings. I was looking for strong, capable women and science fiction was the only place I could find such women. I think [other] women writers and I want to rewrite the endings" (interview, Sept. 2, 1984). Many women science fiction writers acknowledge that they were introduced to science fiction through the pulps, and many began reading them in the 1940s and 1950s, the period during which Jones and Finlay were preeminent illustrators. Le Guin says that she read science fiction magazines as a child (Bucknall 5), and Vinge has asserted that, readers' polls notwithstanding, women have always read science fiction (letter from Vinge, Apr. 5, 1984). Vinge's comment is supported by Butler's description of her introduction to science fiction: "I started reading the magazines—that was my way into adult science fiction. I didn't like them very much, but I kept reading them."[6] James Tiptree, Jr. (Alice Sheldon), told Charles Platt that "she had been reading science fiction since she was ten years old" (266), which suggests that she was influenced by the pulps. Charnas acknowledges, "I read a lot of F & SF [fantasy and science fiction] as a kid" ("Mostly" 8).

Speaking of the covers of pulp magazines, Geoffrey O'Brien asserts that "such art . . . has a way of permeating its surroundings, and of affecting even those barely conscious that they perceive it" (10). His emphasis on the effect of art on viewers is paralleled by reader-response theories. Explaining the importance of reading on writers, Madonne M. Miner cites Norman Holland's theories about reader interaction with texts: "Readers *unconsciously* engage the text for the sake of the pleasure of transposing 'primitive wishes and fears into significance and coherence'" (188). Holland's theory, especially through Miner's feminist application of it, helps explain the allure of science fiction for its female readership. Male readers might be drawn to pulp science fiction by Oedipal fears, but women readers could produce resistant interpretations of the same texts, and some of those readers could then produce texts that developed this resistance more explicitly. In *The Creation of Tomorrow: Fifty Years of Magazine Science Fiction,* Paul A. Carter identifies the period from 1950 on as a time when gender stereotypes were weakening in pulp science fiction, and he explains their impact by referring to the arrival of a new generation of women writers (185).

Whatever the motivation of the pulp reader, pulp science fiction itself is an important part of the historical development of the genre which proved particularly helpful to feminist writers. Fuller's comment, O'Brien's analysis, and Miner's theoretical explanation make explicit the significance of these pulp science fiction magazines and their illustrations.

Pulp cover art is worthy of our attention, not only because it provides the material that feminist science fiction writers were influenced by and subsequently reworked, but also because both cover art and stories contain images of women on which feminist critics draw. Not surprisingly, these female aliens are cast in the image of Frankenstein's monster's mate as well as in the image of mythical female creatures such as the witch or the Medusa. These aliens realize the French feminist theorists' call for the reclamation of the mysterious and uncontrollable feminine. Like Hélène Cixous and Catherine Clément's *Newly Born Woman,* the newly created female alien in pulp science fiction draws on an ambivalent strength from hysterical laughter, seduction, and guilt. As Clément argues about a paranoiac crime, "the hysteric/sorceress uses her own body to enact rebellion, compelling the male viewer/voyeur to watch repeatedly" (Cixous and Clément 18). Her description provides a model for reinterpreting the actions of female aliens in the pulps. Despite their eventual subordination to the male characters, the female aliens present an alternative to science through their bodies, which are larger than life, powerful, overwhelming, even immortal. In the stories, controlling the female alien is a way of controlling the abject, the unknown, the terrifying. As Kristeva explains, the power of horror has been identified as feminine and generative. The abject, she argues, stems from "the demonical power of the feminine" (65, 70) and "fear of the archaic mother turns out to be essentially fear of her generative power" (77). The female alien's reproductive primacy emphasizes the dependency of man on woman. As Clément explains, "It all comes back to man who goes through a woman to reach immortality" (Cixous and Clément 56). Pulp science fiction focuses on issues identified by feminist theorists and reinforces, then works to destroy, the idea of feminine power.

In these science fiction stories, a male character achieves sexual gratification at the cost of a female alien's life, as in Farmer's "Lovers," or his life and the life of patriarchal civilization is secured by a female alien who uses her powers, as in Paul W. Fairman's "Invasion from the Deep." Female aliens "write the body" by altering its size and adapting its powers to a less-robust patriarchal symbolic order. The fact that the female aliens cannot easily fit into the male symbolic order emphasizes the constraints of patriarchy and points to alternatives based on a differently constructed notion of femininity. Before their gigantic bodies are destroyed, these female aliens laugh and expose the weakness of traditional science. These monstrous female bodies defy conventional descriptions and hierarchization of Nature, and they dwarf the hard, technological apparatus of patriarchal science. In their final act of self-destruction, the female aliens of pulp science fiction confirm Kristeva's notion of woman as negation. Through their presence, they evoke the vision of Shelley, who depicted a female PLAGUE that obliterates a patriarchal culture. Pulp science fiction aliens also look forward to contemporary feminist science fiction, like Lessing's Canopus in Argos series, in which a feminine empire offers the only alternative to a rigidly constructed patriarchal symbolic order.

A feminist theoretical vision of the present as mediating a past in which women were powerful and demonic and a future that rediscovers these powers perfectly fits pulp science fiction. Different as date and concerns may be in feminist and pulp redactions, their structures show startling similarities. In pulp science fiction stories and cover art, the male characters encounter female characters with mythic powers. The possibility of the female alien as a speaking subject, even if demonized, empowers later writers, just as Clément and Cixous elaborate their feminist texts from Freud and *Maleficarum,* a misogynist treatise on witchcraft. Feminist science fiction writers acknowledge reading the pulps, and as I demonstrate in later chapters, these images of women emerge transformed in the feminist fictions that followed. This complex reconfiguration of misogynist sources and the reclamation of their images of women shows the sophisticated ways in which feminist theorists can read and reread texts.[7] In this light, pulp science fiction has a more protofeminist configuration than any critic has acknowledged.[8]

Pulp science fiction is one of the "stones available in the house" of patriarchy; and, wisely, feminist science fiction writers have not hesitated to use these stones against the house or even as the material for new texts. One particularly popular version of pulp science fiction art draws upon the mate for Frankenstein's monster in order to create female aliens whose extraordinary strength, size, and ability to reproduce threaten patriarchal order in a way the original solitary male monster could not. In pulp science fiction, however, the female aliens also have the power of Frankenstein: they frequently practice strange magical sciences that present alternatives to traditional hard science.

Despite its immense popularity and influence, pulp science fiction has been ignored by critics. Unfortunately, even the study of science fiction has

been affected by the desire of New Criticism to categorize and create hierarchies that has resulted in a canon of approved texts. This chapter (and the
book in general) breaks down traditional canonization by including pulp
science fiction *and* Le Guin *and* Lessing.[9] Pulp science fiction also minimiz-
es the division (elsewhere maintained in this study) between male and female writers (although Leigh Brackett's work is demonstrably more feminist, as is discussed later in this chapter). Instead the primary emphasis here
is on the breakdown of distinctions between literary and visual texts. What
holds these texts together is the depiction of woman. Rather than being simplistic and readily interpreted, pulp science fiction, especially in the inter-
textuality between the cover art and the literary text, demands a new type
of interpretation, one that draws on literary criticism and on new theories of
the visual. Feminist theory produces a new reading of these texts, one that
helps explain why so many feminist writers are turning to science fiction.
Representative examples of cover art and stories illuminate the overtly sexual nature of the material and the covert feminist possibilities of this depiction of Woman.

An all-female race, "*immortal* . . . worshipped as goddesses . . . [women
who] became the repositories of wisdom, wealth and power" and who venerated the "Great Mother"—this description is not from a novel by Russ,
Charnas, Elgin, or any other contemporary feminist science fiction writer.
Surprisingly, those words were written by a man in 1952. Philip José Farmer's *lalitha* are by no means the first powerful female aliens in science fiction. Thomas Clareson and Sam Moskowitz both trace the depiction of all-
female worlds and worlds ruled by women far back into the nineteenth
century. As their scholarship and twentieth-century representations of female aliens suggest, science fiction's long-standing and well-developed tradition of powerful female aliens points to gender-based anxieties about
women, especially women and science. Through their imposing physical
presences, their reproductive powers, and their alternative science, these
female aliens challenge the dominance of human men. Farmer and other
writers quite certainly did not intend their aliens to provide feminist examples, but their female aliens point the way to contemporary extrapolations
of science fiction's egalitarian possibilities.

Science fiction critics and feminist critics need to examine rather than
dismiss the pulps' depiction of women. True, science fiction's excesses and
sins against women are many, as Le Guin ("American SF"; "Mrs. Brown"),
Beverly Friend ("Virgin Territory"), and others have documented. Many of
the stories from the golden age of science fiction do depict women stereo-

typically and unattractively. Nevertheless, much pulp science fiction depicts strong, independent women in both text and illustrations; indeed, there is much to delight feminist readers in copies of *Planet Stories* and *Fantastic*. Auerbach, in *Woman and the Demon,* demonstrates that, in Victorian fiction, illustrations often provide a vivid key to subtleties in the texts. Focusing on the visual texts is a part of a long-standing tradition among feminist critics that has proved useful for exposing certain kinds of issues that remain covert in literary texts. Similarly, "reading" pulp cover art illuminates the codedly feminist nature of portrayals of women in science fiction. To read pulp science fiction stories without acknowledging their packaging produces a partial and incomplete reading. Similarly, reading feminist science fiction in conjunction with the pulp tradition provides a complete and coherent context because the science fiction magazines of the late 1940s and early 1950s contain portrayals of women that paved the way for the feminist heroines of the 1970s and 1980s.

We can grasp the radical potential of the female aliens from the pulps through the analyses of the depiction of women offered by Simone de Beauvoir and Adrienne Rich. Beauvoir stresses that "woman is a womb" (xv) according to the common stereotype, and Rich emphasizes that motherhood, "the magical power invested in women by men," is manifested "in the form of Goddess-worship or the fear of being controlled and overwhelmed by women" (xv). Both manifestations appear repeatedly in pulp science fiction magazines. In these fictions and artwork, a towering, magically endowed woman struggles with a much smaller, technologically supported man. The size and language of the illustrations and descriptions reflect and evoke male fear of the female as mother, as reproducer, as an all-powerful being.

Because these depictions of anxiety about Woman stress her power, they are nascently feminist. For example, the cover art for "A World He Never Made" by Edward Benson is a science fiction Pieta, with copy to match. The depiction of the maternal through the female alien reaches its height in this painting by Robert Jones, as it reverses the stereotypical depiction of a woman in the arms of a monster. Here, a female monster cradles a human male. Their relationship is of mother to a child—until he rescues her planet and begins to grow to reach her height. At the end of the story, she has been reduced to a nurse, while he becomes "more of a man than he had been" (Benson 38). While the reference to the Madonna is clear in the cover art, in the text the human male recovers and marries the giant female alien. The cover stresses the image of feminine power and authority, symbolized by the necklace and belt she wears: both contain phallic elements, particularly the collar, which, arrowlike, directs the viewer's attention toward the female alien's face. She inevitably invites comparison to the mythical Amazons, who bared their breasts, the better to fight. Even though this female hero tactfully hides her nakedness with the inert male body, her strength prevails. Clasped in her arms, the hero of the title seems unlikely to save anyone or anything. Instead, the female alien appears to have rescued him, a role reversal typical of the pulp stories.

Pulp science fiction stories with strong female aliens often evoke Freud's Oedipus complex as the hero wrestles with a forbidden and usually impossible desire for the maternally minded female alien. The female's size and reproductive powers separate her from humanity and isolate her from the male hero. Pulp science fiction, different in degree if not kind from fiction of the nineteenth century, emphasizes the feminine and may reflect increased masculine anxiety about mothering in each time period—an anxiety about women that can be expressed in Jungian as well as Freudian terms. Erich Neumann, a Jungian analyst, explains that the feminine "becomes everywhere a revered principle of nature, on which man is dependent in pleasure and pain"; he describes "this eternal experience of man, who is as helpless in his dependence on nature as the infant in his dependence on his mother" (129–31).[10] Neumann suggests the importance of mothering for cultures as well as individuals. Like pulp science fiction writers, however, he privileges the male model; that is, he emphasizes the importance of the male integrating the female principle and then neglects the real woman, as Farmer does in "The Lovers."

In "The Lovers" and other pulp science fiction, sexuality is the only way to control these all-powerful female figures. The female alien is self-abnegating; she destroys herself for a man, often willingly. In "The Lovers," the female alien's death reaffirms male dominance. Farmer's Hugo Award–winning short story depicts a female alien who literally succumbs to male potency. The *lalitha* are an insectoid species, matrilineal and matriarchal, immortal unless impregnated. The alien Jeannette falls in love with a man who replaces her birth control drink with an ineffective substitute and she dies horribly as her larvae eat their way out of her abdomen. This demise reflects the anxiety seen earlier in "Mother": fear of being trapped in the womb. Farmer exculpates the man by having the dying Jeannette apologize for not trusting her lover. Ultimately, Jeannette's powers and her ghastly death support Rich's interpretation of misogyny as rooted in "the force of the idea of *dependence on a woman for life itself,* the son's constant effort to assimilate, compensate for or deny the fact that he is 'of woman born' " (xiii).

Jeannette's death might be regarded as a tragic error, except that Farmer's handling of the *lalitha* undercuts this interpretation. Jeannette and the other *lalitha* do have remarkable abilities, but the price for such power is high. She is denied the individuality and independence that Hal discovers through his relationship with her. Despite their powers, or perhaps because of them, the *lalitha* cannot achieve the freedom that is Hal's reward for breaking from his authoritarian society. Hal does not lose everything when Jeannette dies because he has the children a friend claims Jeannette wanted to give him. Furthermore, unlike Hal, Jeannette can be replaced by her relatives; as his friend reminds him, "And there will be women for you. You forget that she has aunts and sisters. All young and beautiful" (63). In this text, fear of a powerful community of women devolves into a literal representation of all women as interchangeable and joined in insecthood.

The weakness of this feminine civilization—that their reproductive capability keeps the *lalitha* subordinate—is revealed in Jeannette's horrible death, which negates her powers of allure. Despite their tremendous sexual attraction and virtual immortality, the *lalitha* fail to maintain their status as goddesses. Like Roger Vadim's film heroine Barbarella, Jeannette is a masculine fantasy of women. Her incredible "natural" beauty and passivity make her the perfect wife. This alien simulacrum has more feminine looks and appeal than human females, an irony Farmer stresses by having his male hero desert his frigid human wife before he leaves for Jeannette's planet. "In the *lalitha* Nature wrote the complete female" (59), a model Farmer implies human women should emulate. Most important, the powerful female alien is subordinate to the human male. Unfortunately, Jeannette's fate represents the situation of most female aliens, and her depiction is further undercut because her race's tremendous powers are not revealed until she lies dying.

Despite the misogynistic plot of "The Lovers," the concept of the *lalitha* prepares us for feminist aliens. The details Farmer chooses for the *lalitha* are exactly those that feminist historians, critics, and writers depict decades later. If the text undercuts the *lalitha* powers, Finlay's illustrations for "The Lovers" stress female power.[11] One of his illustrations depicts the human male apprehensively mesmerized by the female alien, who towers over him. Her scant attire hints at her sexual powers, while the leaves entwining her hair suggest simultaneously her fecundity and her natural powers. Her smile of enticement or glee shows no hint of their relationship's disastrous outcome for her. Jeannette appears to be a part of nature, while her lover (and presumably mankind) is defined by technology, the car that seems to offer him protection or refuge from the female.

The use of technology fits nineteenth-century science fiction's obsession with science as a means of controlling women and protecting men from them. The damage to the front of the car evokes the specter of sexuality's disruption of the masculine refuge in technology. The top of the dashboard is twisted into a curiously revealing phallic shape that seems to be moving toward Jeannette. In a sexually suggestive gesture, the boughs of the tree reach out and cover the hood of the car. Jeannette's absorption of the male hero seems imminent and unavoidable. Her blurry outlines also hint at her metamorphic power because she seems to be a spirit rather than a mortal being. Finlay's illustration emphasizes the power of the female alien, not her inevitable downfall in Farmer's text. But at least the *lalitha* represent a minimal progression from Shelley's *Frankenstein,* in which the female alien is not even given so brief a life.

There are a number of stories whose plots follow "The Lovers" and whose illustrations repeat the emphasis on feminine strength. Most of these have been forgotten; neither the stories nor their protofeminist illustrations are preserved in the many illustrated histories of science fiction. Nevertheless, these female aliens are found in all the pulp magazines, and the patterns they represent deserve our critical attention.[12]

Robert Gibson Jones's cover for *Fantastic Adventures* (May 1951) illustrates a scene from Fairman's "Invasion from the Deep." The large Amazonian woman astride the galfin, or seahorse, appears to be ready to pierce the hapless men on the submarine. The trident symbolizes her power: thrust out from her hip, it embodies her position as a phallic mother, a quality emphasized by the shape of her sea horse, which looms large and rises from between her legs. Little wonder the extremely diminutive male figures have their arms outstretched in horror and disbelief. Their machine gun is hopelessly inadequate compared to the enormous phallus this woman wields. As in the illustration to "The Lovers," where the female alien is associated with Nature, natural appurtenances like the gigantic sea horse dwarf the puny mechanistic phallus of the men. Twenty feet tall, Llanni is one of a race who lives underwater. She is captured by the men and imprisoned in a large tank at sea bottom. In addition to her physical powers, Llanni has the power to stun Nick, the hero, into speechlessness through her beauty. Her captor is a megalomaniac who hopes to rule the world and who has also captured Nick. When a rebellion ensues, Llanni easily frees herself. However, like Farmer's Jeannette, this powerful female alien is slain by love. Llanni can return to her civilization in the depths of the ocean, but she decides to rescue Nick. Bringing him to the surface costs her her life, but she dies happy.

GREAT SCIENCE-FANTASY BY LEADING WRITERS!

fantastic
ADVENTURES

MAY
25¢

A weird and deadly crew planned an . . .

INVASION FROM THE DEEP By PAUL W. FAIRMAN

In the story, the existence of Llanni's race explains the reports of mermaids and emphasizes how little of nature is truly controlled by man. "'The sea is an ancient and mysterious mother,'" one of the characters explains (36). References to mothering appear frequently in the descriptions of female aliens and is connected to Nature, which is depicted as female, mysterious, uncontrollable, and as threatening as Llanni and her galfin. Llanni exudes sexual appeal of a hopeless nature, as this phallic image already suggests. She and Nick are irrevocably separated by her size and their environments. In the text, Llanni is naked; the caviar bedecking her on the cover art was added for decency's sake. All the men who see Llanni desire her. The sexual overtones are emphasized by an in-text illustration by Finlay, as well as by her willingness to assign her phallic power to men: when Llanni meets Nick, she is naked, holding up a phallic submarine on which Nick perches.

Llanni is potentially a feminist heroine because of her size and strength, but the most powerful being in the story is destroyed by her feminine susceptibility for love. In their hysterical and self-destructive passions, such female aliens evoke Cixous and Clément's hysteric-sorceress. Like Finlay's illustrations for "The Lovers," Jones's cover for "Invasion from the Deep" gives no hint of Llanni's downfall. It suggests that women are immensely powerful, while the written text reassures the male reader that women can be reduced to a manageable size by their willingness to sacrifice themselves for men. Again, this discrepancy is typical of the genre, perhaps suggesting a classic set-up; readers may have expected to enjoy the defeat of the formidable woman on the cover.

Robert Jones's painting for "Queen of the Ice Men," depicting a giant alien, a female space captain, shares many of the qualities of the cover art for "The Lovers" and "Invasion from the Deep." But it is particularly interesting in that it is an example of the centrality of science fiction illustrations in the pulps. In this and many other cases, the cover art was created before the story; the writer, S. M. Tenneshaw (a Ziff-Davis house name), tailored the text to fit the artwork. Zetys, the scantily clad and curvaceous female, towers over the diminutive male figures. Like Llanni, she is armed with a weapon of prodigious size, though it is her own size, rather than that of her weapon, that prompts her confident stance. One hand on her hip and the other resting on her weapon, this queen has no fear of the pint-sized men she confronts. As her impressively iron-clad breasts suggest, she is impregnable. She is virtually immortal, a member of a matriarchal culture. Stranded on Earth, she has commanded her spaceship and her crew's descendants for a thousand years. As she gazes down at the miniature (from her perspective) men, she looks irate. One of them is stretched unconscious on the ground, and the other, rope in hand, looks up at her as though expecting orders or destruction. His line of sight is directly linked to hers and he appears mesmerized. Her power and connection to nature are stressed by her scanty attire; she needs little protection against the cold, while the men are covered from head to toe, yet still inadequately protected (as suggested by the unconscious form).

Zetys's extraordinary qualities enable her to survive in the inhospitable Arctic. Like Llanni, she thrives in an area dangerous to man. Like Llanni, she provides a science fiction reproduction of a myth—Zetys is a version of the Snow Queen. Her extraordinary power over nature makes the efforts of the male explorers seem puny; but despite her powers, by the story's conclusion she is reduced both literally and figuratively—she is really no larger than a man, and she needs a man's help when she faces a rebellion. In the end, her main function appears to be to effect a reconciliation between the hero and his hostile superior officer. The cover painting gives no hint of the ending which is so reassuring to the masculine ego. The two men appear completely at Zetys's mercy, one of them overwhelmed by her formidable breasts. Their paralysis visualizes Rich's and Kristeva's depiction of maternal power. The cover art also emphasizes how sexual desire may provide a means for women to control men. In this sense, the painting can be read as a subversive clue to the dangers of glorifying women as sex objects.

Jones is one of the finest science fiction illustrators of women, but by no means is he the only one. The cover of *Planet Stories* often displayed women of Amazonian proportions hovering over diminutive men, as did the cover painting by Malcolm Smith for the first issue of *Other Worlds* (November 1949), which illustrates "The Fall of Lemuria" by Richard S. Shaver. Like many other pulp science fiction writers, Shaver asserts the importance of female Nature. Maiya is enormous, some forty feet tall (or long, depending on how you view her). She is beautiful, brave, intelligent, and powerful. On the cover, she is shown gleefully striking down a much smaller male. The illustration exudes energy, and the phallic imagery is pervasive and compelling: the lines of the sword, dragon, the lamia herself, all direct the reader's attention toward Maiya's commanding presence. The images are explicitly sexual, from her own snake shape, to the sword she wields, to the hair standing up on end on the little male figure. The backdrop of a tunnel and her curvaceous breasts, tastefully hidden by her hair, make it clear that this is a female alien. She appears to be enjoying, even relishing, her pow-

OTHER WORLDS

SCIENCE STORIES

November 1949 35c

FIRST ISSUE

THE FALL OF LEMURIA

By RICHARD S. SHAVER

WHERE NO FOOT WALKS by G. H. IRWIN

VENUS TROUBLE SHOOTER by JOHN WILEY

ers. In the story itself, Shaver employs ostensibly factual narration; he insists that human legends are memories of dead civilizations, thus unintentionally supporting feminist claims of prepatriarchal, matriarchal civilizations. This protofeminist background asserts a civilization-wide context of mothering—again, perhaps, prompted by the larger culture's glorification of mothers.

In another version of feminine power, Barye Phillips and L. R. Summers's cover painting for "The Opal Necklace" by Kris Neville (a male writer) stresses the metamorphic quality of the female alien. Naked writhing female bodies dominate the composition of the witch's hair, recalling the Medusa. The hair and the various colors in the portrait emphasize female power to entrance through sexuality and female power to metamorphose. The woman depicted on the cover is at the same time a powerful witch and a young, beautiful woman in love, a mother and a daughter around whom the story centers. Neville emphasizes the mother's power; the first words of the story are, "Yes, Mother," a refrain repeated throughout. The daughter asks her mother to cast a spell over her future husband, but, once married, the daughter feels trapped. When the mother uses mysterious powers to free herself, the daughter dies, killing herself instead of her husband. In the cover art, however, the witch seems to hypnotize as she glares out at the reader, a bowl of blood in her hands. This alien has no hint of pleasure; rather, she exudes unabashed menace. Most tellingly, her gaze is directed toward the presumably male consumer of the magazine. The blood suggests female reproductive capacity and hints at violence. At the same time, this female alien evokes the life-giving power of women; she appears to generate dozens of people in her hair. Her serpents are not phallic because of their multiplicity but are instead a new version of the lamia: women as snakes. In the cover art, the feminine potential for reproduction becomes explicitly dangerous and fearsome. Ironically, the story contains no births, only the female protagonist's death, despite her magical powers.

While most of the pulp writers and artists were men, one of the few women writers revised the misogynistic ending of the formula. As the cover for Leigh Brackett's "Black Amazon of Mars" demonstrates, woman science fiction writers could embellish the portrait of the strong female alien. In this case, as in many other pulp magazine paintings, the art depicts an actual scene from the story. This character and illustrations of her clearly belong with the others discussed in this chapter, yet there are significant differences that hint at the transformation of science fiction by later women writers. In F. Anderson's painting,[13] the Amazon dominates the cover, swinging ag-

gressively—at first glance, apparently at the reader. In the background, lower left, John Stark is engulfed by the predatory fronds, evoking in their tendrils that often depicted, dangerous siren Nature. Overwhelmed by Nature, Stark must let his female companion wage the fight more effectively than he can. His figure is dwarfed by that of the Amazon, Ciara, whose sexual characteristics are emphasized by the form-fitting metal outfit. Again, in the competition between phallic objects, Ciara wins: her ax is larger and more commanding than the ineffectually wielded sword Stark holds in one hand. However, her thrusting breasts, parted lips, and vagina-evoking belt buckle all remind the viewer that Ciara is most emphatically feminine—though perhaps a heroine who is far less a part of nature than the other female aliens in pulp science fiction. Her armored body separates her from the plantlike monster far more than Stark, whose bare chest is engulfed by the threatening tentacles. Ciara's tremendous foregrounding dwarfs Stark in ways quite unlike the other illustrations; she is not focused on him but rather upon their common enemy.

This illustration points toward the way Brackett's story differs from those by male science fiction writers. Unlike them, she does not cast her hero and heroine's relationship in terms of a mother-son bond, and she does not even mention Ciara's reproductive capacity. At the end of the story, Ciara will rule the city she has conquered, and Stark agrees to remain with her, at least for a while. In contrast to other textual depictions of female aliens and men, Brackett's vision embraces a union without diminishing the woman. At the conclusion, as well as the beginning of the story, Stark is silenced by Ciara's "strength and splendor" (108). Here, then, is a female alien whose formidable powers evoke the maternal and the metamorphic but who escapes the formulaic ending in which she is usually destroyed. Brackett's revision of the misogynist plot remains close enough to the formula to be publishable, even as it points to the more radical revisionings of female aliens that later twentieth-century feminists would create.

All these examples show that male and female pulp writers *and* artists are an important part of the heritage of contemporary woman science fiction writers. Studying the pulp magazines reveals science fiction's fascination with the figure of the woman. Male science fiction writers did exclude human women from their texts, but they represented the feminine through the female alien. These woman are initially powerful and threatening and thrust their sex aggressively toward the reader and the men in the stories. But by the end of the texts, the female is put in her proper place, subordinate to the male characters. Her subordination is even justified by the sexual or physical threat she poses to mankind.

STRANGE ADVENTURES ON OTHER WORLDS

MARCH, 25¢

PLANET
stories

TRADE MARK REG.

A.N.C.

A hooded war-lord led
the hordes of Mekh
against the Ancient Doom...

BLACK AMAZON
of MARS

A Novel of Warrior Worlds
by LEIGH BRACKET

THE STAR-SAINT *by* A. E. VAN VOGT

FYFE • GALLUN • ANDERSON

This inevitable denouement is not depicted in the illustrations that capture the drama and the potential of the stories' emphasis on the female alien. If male science fiction writers were unable to extrapolate the egalitarian possibilities of the genre, the pulp writers developed a depiction of woman that was readily transformed by contemporary feminist writers. Norton's witches draw on the visual and the textual description of Farmer's *lalitha*. Vinge's Snow Queen is a direct descendant of Tenneshaw's "Queen of the Ice Men." And McIntyre's Snake is a revamping of Shaver's lemuria. In these and other rewritings of pulp science fiction stories and art, feminist writers retain the depiction of female strength and reject the pessimistic ending of the texts.

Because the pulp magazine is a part of science fiction tradition, its paradigms are what many feminist science fiction writers know best. Studying pulp science fiction reveals that feminist writers are able to draw on specific generic qualities of science fiction to create their heroines. Feminist science fiction can then be read as a developing strand of the genre that always focused on women, and the emergence of feminist writing in the genre is thus more properly viewed as a logical growth instead of a bizarre and inexplicable aberration. Only by examining pulp magazines can we realize the extent of the feminist legacy bequeathed to feminists. Through their portraits of powerful female aliens, science fiction artists helped to keep alive the notion of female empowerment. As the next two chapters demonstrate, the female aliens in these pictures erupt from the confines of the pulp science fiction frames as contemporary women writers fully realize the potential of the earlier pulp female aliens.

Notes

1. Many writers have discussed these years and their effect on their writing (e.g., Del Rey, *The World of Science Fiction;* Asimov, *The Early Asimov*). For an overview of magazine science fiction, see Carter, *The Creation of Tomorrow.*

2. In her discussion of *She,* Auerbach points out that Ayesha has powers of "magical metamorphoses beyond the capacities of the strongest male" and that since Ayesha's source of power is "Nature consistently personified as female . . . the queen is not only magic, but the holy source of her own magic" (*Demon* 36, 38–39). This paradigm applies to female aliens, of which Ayesha is one of the most famous.

3. Darko Suvin was among the first to recognize this feminist aspect of *Flatland.*

In *Victorian Science Fiction* Suvin claims that "Abbott's astoundingly radical vision [of a male double standard] . . . is unmatched in English-language SF until the modern feminists" (372).

4. James Gunn writes, "In 1949 the eruption of new magazines began" (161), and he titles a chapter in *Alternate Worlds* "The Big Boom: 1940–1955."

5. This was accompanied by the comcommitant expansion of the pin-up girl into a sexual idol (e.g., Marilyn Monroe) and was later criticized by feminists and analyzed by historians.

6. Butler made this comment at the "Single Pro Session" at the Forty-second World Science Fiction Convention, Anaheim, California, August 30, 1984. In an interview, she goes into further detail: "My first experience with adult SF came through the magazines at the grocery store. Whenever I could afford them I'd buy copies of *Amazing* and *Fantastic*" (qtd. in McCaffery 59).

7. As Annette Kuhn argues, "meanings . . . are circulated between representation, spectator and social formation" (6). She makes this observation about film, but her work echoes and supports Cixous and Clément's notions about the relationship between the male spectator and the female paranoiac/alien.

8. *Protofeminist* refers to those qualities in the stories and art that are the progenitors of contemporary feminist science fiction. It means containing characteristics that resemble modern feminist ideas, but in a primitive or undeveloped form. Unconsciously, pulp science fiction writers and artists created female characters who are potentially feminist heroines, as I demonstrate in this chapter.

9. Because Lessing is rarely discussed as a science fiction writer, her inclusion in this book signifies a breakdown of traditional categories.

10. Significantly, Neumann's book was first published during the early 1950s, the same time as pulp science fiction, which reflects a similar view in fiction. Like the work of pulp science fiction writers, Neumann's work is protofeminist. Rich draws on his scholarship in *Of Woman Born*.

11. The *Startling Stories* cover art, by Earle K. Bergey, represents Jeannette and the male hero in a conventional embrace. This portrait is atypical, while Finley's internal illustrations are more representative of the story and of the depictions of female aliens.

12. A partial listing of other magazine covers with similiar art: *Amazing* 23 (May 1949); 21 (May 1947); 23 (October 1949); 22 (August 1948); 22 (March 1948); *Fantastic* 10 (December 1948); 11 (March 1949); 10 (April 1948); 14 (August 1952); 9 (September 1947); 9 (October 1947).

13. I have been unable to determine whether F. Anderson is male or female.

THREE

Feminist Utopias

While male writers and artists did bequeath an important legacy to feminist writers, women writers left a more substantial bequest, the feminist utopia—a gift that has not been fully placed in the context of the history of science fiction.[1] There is a large and important body of criticism on the feminist utopia by Lee Cullen Khanna, Carol Farley Kessler, Frances Bartkowski, and others, but the territory needs to be re-covered in this book to have a full history of the feminine in science fiction. Because the feminist utopia is a critical category unto itself, this chapter provides an overview and should not be considered comprehensive. Rereading the feminist utopias provides background and perspective for the feminist science fiction that follows the utopias. Historically and ideologically, feminist utopias represent a midpoint between the early science fiction dystopias and later feminist science fiction. Through the notion of a utopia, a world that is both perfect and nonexistent, feminist writers create a separate space for women. From Lane's *Mizora* to Charnas's *Motherlines,* feminist utopias enact the strategy of separatism through alternative science, a reworking of myths about mothering and the valorization of qualities identified as feminine: an emphasis on community, home, and family. This paradigm functions in response to male-dominated science fiction.

Separatism binds together nineteenth- and twentieth-century feminist utopias, as Auerbach points out when she comments that " 'the great-minded over-mothers' of Herland are the staunch progenitors of such contemporary female Utopias as Joanna Russ's evanescent Whileaway" (*Communities* 163). Nineteenth-century feminist utopias begin with a rigidly exclusionary stance: they cannot imagine a space for men in their worlds and they are racist as well. Yet they are worth considering, especially in contrast to male dystopias, for women writers present a more humane version of genetics used by male writers (Albinski, *Women's Utopias* 27). By the twentieth century, however, the feminist utopia demonstrates a more truly feminist inclusionary politics that focuses on race, class, and gender in varying degrees.

The twentieth-century feminist utopia broadens its scope, as Bartkowski explains: "The shift in perspective from the late nineteenth- to late twentieth-century utopian critiques is the shift from capitalism and its discontents to patriarchy" (9). Although later utopias are more open, one strand of the twentieth-century feminist utopia keeps alive separatism and the anger that prompts it. While they separate themselves from the male-dominated world, feminist utopias attempt to bring women together.

From the nineteenth century to the present, the utopias exemplify what Carol Gilligan describes as the impact of feminism, which encourages women to valorize relationships and community "as a source of moral strength" (149). In moral dilemmas, women's "different voice" values interdependence over independence, feeling over thinking, mercy over justice (23, 69). Gilligan's subjects stress cooperation and participants in her study emphasize not "how to lead a moral life without interfering with the rights of others" but "how 'to lead a moral life which includes obligations to myself and my family and people in general'" (21). In the feminist utopia, countries, worlds, and even universes are ruled and improved by feminine values that emphasize the domestic and familial. In her study of utopias, Carol Farley Kessler discovered that, "Typically, women [utopian writers] make issues of family, sexuality, and marriage more central than do men" (7). Similarly, Russ describes feminist utopias and adds that they are also "classless, without government, ecologically minded . . . *sexually permissive*" (Russ, *Amor* 76). The feminist utopia does not have compulsory heterosexuality or homosexuality but instead is pro-choice and consequently often contains a variety of sexual relationships, reflecting the liberty so treasured in the feminist vision. In these ideal female communities, the full range of human activities is open to women.

As you read a feminist utopia, you remove yourself from the setting of patriarchal society and its suppositions. Creating feminist utopias, then, involves the practice of "stepping abruptly outside and . . . affirming absolute rupture" that Derrida describes, and it also involves "chang[ing] ground in a discontinuous and eruptive manner" (56). Unlike the female dystopias so beloved in traditional science fiction, feminist utopias initially depend on physical isolation and cataclysm to protect them from patriarchy—the pervasiveness and destructive power of which is emphasized by their physical inaccessibility. By creating worlds without men, as in Gilman's *Herland,* or worlds without immutable categories of gender, as in Le Guin's *Left Hand of Darkness,* feminist utopian writers disavow the structure of the patriarchal world as well as that of the female dystopia. In place of capitalism, feminist science fiction offers a communal version of the home as model for an ideal society.[2] By stressing values identified as feminine, the genre of feminist utopias functions as a radical experiment in thought and as a rigorous challenge to existing social patterns.

Feminist utopias, idealized all-female or female-ruled worlds, have a history of their own that dates back to medieval times—for example, Christine de Pizan's *Book of the City of Ladies* (1405). It was in the nineteenth century, however, that the feminist utopia flourished in English literature. While Bulwer-Lytton and Besant were condemning the New Woman in their female dystopias, woman writers were busy imagining the positive effects of female emancipation. Although feminist utopias constitute a well-established tradition, Kessler correctly points out that "much has been said and written about men's visions of eutopia; we know far less about women's" (7). One reason for this lack of knowledge is that, until recently, feminist utopias have not been available in print. The works of writers like Bulwer-Lytton and Besant have been preserved in university libraries, while those of Gilman and Lane were not even originally published as books but serialized in ephemeral journals. Despite the differences in publication history, the feminist utopia and female dystopia share the same tropes. Although both focus on all-female worlds or worlds ruled by women, they differ dramatically in their interpretation and use of the paradigm of female rulers. While the dystopias are misogynistic and often directed against specific political developments such as women's enfranchisement, the feminist utopia valorizes reproduction, depicts mothering as a justification for female rule, and looks toward idyllic futures brought about by the adoption of feminine values.

By reversing the male dystopian pattern, feminist utopian writers promote women's rights. In these novels, the unwilling male explorer from a female dystopia is transformed into a missionary for a feminist cause. As Carol Pearson notes, "the most common plot structure of the feminist utopian novel is the conversion story in which a male narrator comes to see a feminist society as superior to a male-dominated one" (59). Significantly, the missionary usually becomes a writer and art provides salvation for the feminist. This pattern occurs with male narrators in Gilman's *Herland*, James Schmitz's *Witches of Karres*, Dorothy Bryant's *Kin of Ata Are Waiting for You*, and Le Guin's *Left Hand of Darkness*. The pattern can also mutate with a female protagonist exploring a female utopia, as in Lane's *Mizora*, Charnas's *Motherlines*, and Russ's *Female Man*. The narrator's point of view may vary, but the argument itself remains unchanged: our society is reevaluated when its representative is forced to acknowledge an outsider's perspective.

Because science fiction allows writers to adapt ideas about progress to include women, the feminist utopia provides a blueprint for the future. In addition to encouraging readers to rethink traditional stereotypes, utopias can become, as Kessler stresses, "spiritual guides" (5). These qualities of the utopia explain why it was of particular importance to nineteenth-century women. While Edward Bellamy's *Looking Backward,* like most utopias written by men, did not offer women equality, the tremendous interest generated by the novel and the general utopian hopes of the late nineteenth century undoubtedly spurred women writers to create feminist utopias. Far more radical than *Looking Backward,* feminist utopias reverse the "anti-science, anti-progress" depiction of woman in the dystopias. In their place, feminist utopias offer a vision of the world based on what are identified as feminine values allied with a progressive social order and an alternative science.

Early Feminist Utopias

■ Lane's *Mizora: A Prophecy* (1890)[3] and Gilman's *Herland* (1915) represent the early feminist tradition in their content and publication history; both were neglected until they were reprinted in the 1970s. In their novels, Lane and Gilman create all-female paradises in which women practice science based on feminist values. In the feminist utopia, women are shown to be competent rulers; and their management and understanding of human relations and their skillful combination of science and reproduction enables them to thrive without men. Lane and Gilman reverse the female dystopian tropes of woman alien, woman scientist, and woman ruler and use all-female worlds to argue *for* women's rights. In both *Mizora* and *Herland,* women concentrate on female physiology, a study notoriously neglected by science. Consequently, female "witches" unlock the secrets of life and learn how to control reproduction. While male scientists like Terry, Jeff, and Vandyke in *Herland* explore unknown continents, women explore the world of the mind. As a result, women discover mental powers that seem magical and mysterious from the perspective of traditional science.

The feminist independence that results from psionics appears equally magical to the male explorers in *Mizora* and *Herland.* Both worlds, however, rely on separatism to enable their feminist society's development of a science that opposes and is stronger than traditional male-dominated science, and both rework myths of mothering and emphasize community and home. In each text, physical isolation and the complete absence of men produces the feminist utopia. *Mizora* is set in the Arctic and *Herland* in the tropics; in each case the extreme climate that surrounds the utopia represents the loss of men and testifies to the success of the female societies. The women not only exist without men but prove that women can live comfortably in intemperate climates that are oases. Despite physical isolation, these societies are utopian for women, because in them they can live without patriarchal restrictions. In each story, the self-sufficient society is contacted by an outsider who realizes through the feminist utopia how oppressed women are in the "real" world.

First published serially in a Cincinnati newspaper in 1880–81, *Mizora* was so popular that in the following year it was published in book form. Although little is known about the author (the work was first printed anonymously), it seems likely that she had read *Frankenstein* because the outlines of Shelley's novel are revised in *Mizora* not to show the masculine abuse of science but the appropriate feminine use of those skills. Like Walton, Lane's heroine, Vera, undertakes a trip to the Arctic. She poses as a young man to escape political persecution as an aristocrat in Russia. Stranded in the Arctic, she feels the desire to explore land where "no white man's foot has ever stepped" (12), language remarkably similar to Shelley's, whose narrator hopes to "tread a land never before imprinted by the foot of man" (*Frankenstein* 15). Bereft of family and deserted at the North Pole, Vera discovers the land of Mizora—paralleling the action in *Frankenstein,* where a lonely Walton is threatened with his crew's desertion and meets Frankenstein and his monster. While Walton hopes to discover a new civilization, he fails to discover a utopia and instead meets a monster. Lane's vision is more optimistic, but like Shelley's narrator, her heroine must be prepared to change. As Frankenstein shatters Walton's belief in science, so Mizora challenges Vera's assumptions about male dominance. Mizora is a feminist utopia, a small, scientifically advanced world that reproduces parthenogenetically.

Just as Walton serves as a double for Victor, so Vera's character points to the problems Frankenstein faces and to a feminist solution to those problems. Unlike Frankenstein, who rejects his creation, Mizorans[4] love their children and live idyllically and comfortably with them. Using the same setting as Shelley and similarly emphasizing the loneliness of her protagonist, Lane creates a female Victor Frankenstein and sends her heroine on a fruitful search for love and the perfect society. Where Victor's science leads to sterility and death, Vera discovers science used wisely and humanely to create life, even in the hostile Arctic. This landscape and its lack of contamination by men make it an appropriate setting for a feminist utopia. It is literally, as Elaine Showalter describes a theoretical space for women, a "wild zone . . . the 'mother country' of liberated desire and female authenticity; crossing to the other side of the mirror" (201). At the same time, the feminist exploration and survival in this inaccessible area shows the ambition of the feminist utopia to surpass patriarchal society's achievements, as Victor Frankenstein hopes to rival previous scientific achievements.[5]

Mizora's physical separation from the real world functions as a reproach to the patriarchal society Vera left. Through this utopian society, Lane suggests the rewards of the feminist struggle; though she is lonely and alienated when she returns to the real world, Vera is sustained by the Mizoran way of life. Their powers are remarkable: Mizorans live for hundreds of years and retain youthful beauty and enjoy heightened senses of sight and smell. Most significantly, Mizorans practice parthenogenesis and after thousands of years of reproducing themselves create a race apart. The gradual extinction of "the race of men" (93) has allowed Mizorans to purify their race and to discover the latent female talent for science. While admiring everything she learns about Mizorans, Vera keeps wondering how they have managed all these magnificent achievements without men: "It seemed, therefore, impossible to me for a country or government to survive without his assistance or advice" (20). Mizora belies the superiority of man by its very existence and perfection; in it, the pulp magazine's evil Snow Queen becomes a modern, efficient, and kind ruler. "The State was the beneficent mother who furnished everything" (230) and the aristocracy has been abolished. In this ideal world, there are no wars, no locks or bolts, no crime.

Mizoran society, however, has been purified in a way that reflects racist assumptions, an unfortunate feature of the late nineteenth-century feminist movement (Bammer 9). Although Vera admires the Mizorans and adopts their values, they remain alien, a separate race. Vera has dark hair and a dark complexion; the Mizorans have eradicated all but blonde hair and blue eyes through eugenics, because to the Mizorans, so-called Aryan characteristics are superior. Lane partially defuses the racism by having the change occur gradually, centuries before Vera discovers Mizora. Despite their beliefs, the Mizorans wholeheartedly accept Vera. They pity her not for her genes or coloration but because she has a husband and son. When she finally leaves Mizora, the Preceptress gives her own daughter to be Vera's companion and thus demonstrates the society's acceptance of her. However, though it is partially diffused by the plot, the racism in the novel exposes one of the weaknesses of a utopian approach: while emphasizing difference and separation, the female utopian writer runs the risk of excluding others from the very freedom she creates for her own select group of characters.

The plot of *Mizora* draws on Hans Christian Andersen's "Snow Queen" as well as on Shelley's *Frankenstein*. Literary fairy tales like those of Charles Perrault or Andersen are often myths of female oppression, explanations and justifications for women's subordinate status. Ruling over a world set in the Arctic, and gifted by mysterious and seemingly magical science, the Snow Queen epitomizes the notion of an feminine alternative. Her power is revealed by the young boy, Kay, who is struck by a piece of the distorting mirror and who then ridicules his grandmother's picture book and stories and begins to study snowflakes scientifically with his magnifying glass. Kay brags to the Snow Queen that he "could do mental arithmetic, as far as fractions, and that he knew the number of square miles and the number of inhabitants of the country" (20). He spends his time in the Snow Queen's Palace creating "'Ice Puzzles of Reason'" (61), or abstract computations.

Although it is similarly located in the Arctic and female-ruled, Mizora is a beneficent version of the Snow Queen's kingdom. Lane shows that the distorting mirror is not created by female dominance, as Andersen implies, but by sexism and the practice of hard science. Because the Mizorans use an alternative science wisely and humanely, their land is not a misogynistic prison but a feminist paradise. Andersen valorizes Gerda's nurturing role and condemns the Snow Queen's power. In contrast to attractive Kay, the Snow Queen is frigid and uncaring, a negative role model. Her magic suggests the illicit female power of witches. The Mizorans' science is just as magical, but by associating women with the study and investigation of natural phenomena, Lane asserts female intelligence and capacity to master a "masculine" subject. The Mizorans gain legitimation from the socially acceptable institution of science because Lane uses it to depict Mizora as a world that could actually exist.

Lane presents women as complete mistresses of science; their skills far surpass those of scientists in 1880 and even 1993. Unlike the female aliens of the dystopias, their skills are not procured through sacrifice or traffic with the devil or demons. They are not witches with special powers but women who have studied nature for centuries. In *Mizora,* Lane suggests that women have a strong aptitude for science, a talent that was not developed earlier because of sexism. The book shows the extraordinary capabilities of woman as scientist in a world where females are given the opportunity to exercise their talents. *Mizora* endorses science used by women to create life, rather than the destruction associated with male technology. Mizorans have created bread from stone and have life spans of hundreds of years, lifelong youth, planes, cars, television, and even television phones.

Because the Mizorans use parthenogenesis, science is central to Lane's reworking of mothering. Their form of reproduction is not the cold, dispassionate exogenesis of the female dystopias. Rather, Mizorans love their children and are shocked and disgusted by Vera's mention of forced childbearing. They have children only by choice and spend their long lives in harmony with their daughters. Throughout Mizora, the word "mother" is used in an adulatory fashion. Science and nature, the two benefactresses of Mizora, are constantly referred to as "Mothers." The Preceptress of the National College exalts the primacy of the female when she explains parthenogenesis to Vera: "'Daughter,' she said, solemnly, 'you are now looking upon the germ of *all* Life; we have advanced far enough in Science to control its development. Know that the *Mother* is the only important part of all life'" (103).

This emphasis on women's capacity to bear children typifies early feminist utopias, which are essentialist, like the feminist movements of that time.[6] These fictions rely on a simple reversal of values to create a world that challenges and improves upon patriarchal society. In the process, they create alternative visions of what science could be if it were based on feminine rather than masculine values. However, to create such a world the early feminist utopias had to eradicate men completely.

Better known to contemporary readers than *Mizora* is Gilman's *Herland*. Although it did not appear in book form until 1979, it has been influential, perhaps because the author's message is less militant than Lane's. In contrast to Mizora's self-assertion, Gilman's utopia depends more on circumstance than on female self-advancement. The women of Herland develop parthenogenesis accidentally and naturally after the men die out as a result of war. Lane wrote before the twentieth century, while Gilman wrote during World War I; in the thirty-five years between the two books, the increasing awareness of industrial illnesses and the evil purposes to which technology could be put—chemical and aerial warfare—diminished the hope of science as a savior. Instead of hard science, Gilman stresses social compromise, or the practice of soft science. Finally, as in the female dystopias, one of *Herland's* main characters renounces the utopia for the real world. Although *Herland* is a utopia, its message is less fruitful for feminist science fiction revisionists than is *Mizora,* because Gilman does not provide her utopians with the same scientific ability and self-sufficiency that Lane envisioned.

Like Mizora, Herland is enabled by its isolation. It is a nation without wars, aristocracy, or priests, surrounded by snow-capped mountains and an icy ridge that evokes the frozen world of Demeter's wrath, the Arctic of *Mizora,* "The Snow Queen," and *Frankenstein.* Once again the outsider (from our world) cannot conceive that an isolated female world could be wholly self-sufficient. As the male narrator and his two companions speculate about the nature of "a strange and terrible Woman Land" (2), one of them imagines he will become king of the land because he cannot conceive of women who would not immediately capitulate to male authority. As the men come closer to Herland, the presence of cloth and other artifacts convinces them there must be men in the society. When they see how competently organized the people are, they again insist that only men could manage so well. Their reluctance to accept Herland's autonomy emphasizes how spectacularly the women of Herland have succeeded. Their disbelief is corroborated by the events that enable the utopia—a war in which all the men died. Only after the patriarchy's self-destruction can a feminist utopia exist, and this utopia begins to crumble at the end of the novel. Herland's isolation is less stable than Mizora's, and its breakdown shows one weakness of separatism as a strategy: it is difficult to maintain.

Like Lane, Gilman associates female autonomy with superior mothering, and metaphors of mothering dominate the narrative and Herland's social structure (Freibert 71). The Mizorans' culture focuses on children rather than science; Herland is preeminently a nation of mothers. "Children were the *raison d'etre* in this country" (51), the narrator stresses, and he reduces his tutor to tears when he explains that dogs often bite children where he comes from. The Herlandians' feelings are stronger than the pale emotions of women in patriarchal society, perhaps because all Herlandians are the daughters of one mother—the first to reproduce parthenogenetically. "Motherhood means to us something which I cannot yet discover in any of the countries of which you tell us" (66), the tutor explains. Mother-love is their religion; at first a Mother Goddess, eventually a "Maternal Pantheism. . . . Here was Mother Earth, bearing fruit. All that they ate was fruit of motherhood. . . . By motherhood they were born and by motherhood they lived—life was, to them, just the long cycle of motherhood" (59).

By the end of the novel, however, motherhood becomes problematic. The plot of *Herland* follows the Demeter myth: three of the women are persuaded by the men to marry them and are separated from Herland. At the novel's conclusion, one of them, Ellador, forsakes the "semitropical" Herland for her husband and enters Ourland, the underworld of seasons, war, and patriarchy. Gilman presents Ellador's defection ambiguously; despite her husband's descriptions of the outside world, Ellador does not appreciate the extent of female oppression in Ourland. Nevertheless, Gilman endorses both Ellador's love for her husband and the acceptance of men in Herland, and she describes the invasion of Herland as a fortunate fall, one that will benefit Ourland.

Despite her eventual insistence on integration, Gilman presents a positive depiction of the female alien. The women of Herland appear literally alien; the men have difficulty accepting them as women: "Each was in the full bloom of rosy health, erect, serene, standing sure-footed and light as any pugilist" (20). The sympathetic narrator describes his own wife as a "witch" and a "wonder-woman" and all Herlandians as "women, *plus*" (130, 142, 128). They all have perfect vision and, like the Mizorans, are of "Aryan stock," though "somewhat darker than our northern races because of their constant exposure to sun and air" (54). This description reveals that Gilman too accepted nineteenth-century racist assumptions, and her racial bias reveals again a weakness of utopianism as a strategy. It is a part of a trade-off in which a role reversal (women ruling without men) results in the neglect of the structural similarity between sexism and racism. Gilman's aliens are not truly alien, as later feminist writers depict them, but human women only temporarily isolated from the patriarchy.

Despite the positive depiction of a feminine culture, and the humbling of all three men, by the end of the novel Gilman has moved away from the utopia. The women welcome the men; the woman who marries the narrator concedes, "We are only half a people" (97). "New Woman" originally refers to the parthenogenetic progenitors, but in the end the term is applied to the three women who marry the male intruders. The location of Herland may still be hidden, but the first bisexually conceived child is created, and one of the men stays behind. Herland will not remain the same, nor does it want to. The ominousness of the change is implied by the results of the marriages: one ends after the husband attempts to rape his wife; the other couple leaves; and even the couple expecting a child has marital difficulties. The conclusion of *Herland* falls somewhere between female dystopias, where all-female societies laud any male invader, and feminist utopias, which are self-sufficient. While Gilman's intent is undoubtedly feminist, because her community of women accepts men without a struggle, she does not fully realize the possibilities of the feminist utopia.

Herland shows the dilution of the feminist vision, a vision that lay fallow until the rebirth of feminist utopias some fifty years later. The rapidity of the dissolution of the early feminist utopias shows the need to modify the form. While Gilman was as clearly committed to feminism as was Lane, isolated, all-female utopian communities prove inadequate, even in a text that, like *Mizora,* bears the name of a female utopia. *Herland'*s consciousness of the impermanence of such a community emphasizes the need, even in a feminist utopia, to include men. In this way, the utopias act out the drama of feminism and feminist criticism itself. At first isolationist, feminism and feminist criticism moved toward acknowledging and engaging men, and from focusing on women to focusing on gender.

Twentieth-Century Feminist Utopias

■ The twentieth-century feminist utopias differ from their predecessors in several ways. Fortunately, the overtly racist assumptions that marred the works of Lane and Gilman generally have disappeared. But racism is still a problem feminist utopias and science fiction must confront—and an issue with which their critics must grapple. The development of feminist criticism in the social sciences and literary criticism creates new feminist models for female science fiction writers. Most important, social changes have allowed feminist writers to imagine male characters sympathetic to feminism. The early feminist utopias allow the reader to imagine a place set aside for women and examine that place and what becomes possible in it. Because of their move away from essentialism, one set of later feminist utopias introduces visions of ideal communities that are feminist in character but can include men. The feminist utopias that can incorporate like-minded men also involve a variety of ethnic groups. While one set of later utopias is integrated by sex, another stresses the importance of integrating men and women into power structures, but it does so by threatening men with disaster if they do not share their power. Both responses prepare us for modern feminist science fiction, in which male and female characters can meet as equals. Like their predecessors, twentieth-century feminist utopias draw on an alternative science, rework myths of mothering, and emphasize community and family. They also build on their nineteenth-century antecedents to set up a dialogic frame with feminist and male-dominated science fiction.

One of the first science fiction writers to realize the legacy of Lane and Gilman was James Schmitz,[7] whose assimilationist utopia might be considered a prototype for those that followed. *The Witches of Karres* proves that a writer need not be female to be a feminist, and it points to the breaking down of the rigid separatism of earlier feminist utopias. Instead of being populated only by women, Schmitz's utopian planet also contains men with witchlike powers, including the male protagonist's great uncle. The novel follows the pattern set in the female dystopia and the feminist utopia: a male scientist, a spaceship captain, finds and rescues three young witches and journeys to a planet run by women. The witches entangle the hapless captain in their conflict with the Empire and eventually take him to Karres, where everyone has witchlike powers, though individuals tend to specialize in certain areas: one might practice telekinesis; another, precognition. Because Pausert eventually accepts the witches, he benefits from their powers: he now has the fastest ship in the galaxy, powered by the magical Sheewash Drive. His contact with Karres exposes the stupidity of the Empire's treatment of the witches, whose powers are far superior and far more appealing than those of the totalitarian regime. When threatened by the Empire, the witches concentrate and through communal effort produce enough energy to move their planet. Because of the witches' powers and the planet's female rule, all spaceships are forbidden to land on Karres. The Empire deals with the feminist utopia by exiling it, creating the isolation that feminist utopias require.

Karres's politics, however, demonstrates that, though isolated, a feminist utopia need not exclude men. *The Witches of Karres* reveals an alternative that neither Lane nor Gilman could imagine: a world based on feminist values that are accepted by men. Despite its explicit feminism, Schmitz's book, published only three years before Le Guin's *Left Hand of Darkness,* did not provoke controversy. One reason for this neglect may be the age of Schmitz's protagonists—the witches are children—which allows readers to dismiss the book as a novel for juveniles. Even more damaging, from a political perspective, is the light-hearted tone, which makes the novel enjoyable reading. Captain Pausert is a misfit and a bit of a buffoon. Logically, he is the only person likely to disregard the Empire's ban against Karres because, as an outsider, he has little to lose. However, the comedic aspects of the book may mislead readers into ignoring the truly revolutionary nature of this first contemporary feminist utopia.

While Le Guin's *Left Hand of Darkness* (1969) contains no major women characters, it does stress issues of mothering and relationships. Winter is a feminist utopia, but it differs from its precursors in its inclusiveness in terms of gender, race, and even planet of origin.[8] Like Shelley, Le Guin brilliantly turns female absence into presence through science fiction tropes. She uses the pattern of the male dystopia but reverses its meaning: her male explorer-scientist, Genly Ai, journeys to Winter to convince a planet of uniquely Other aliens to join the Ekumen, the association of planets. The Gethenians are androgynous, and each goes through a sexual phase called "kemmer" in which s/he becomes either male or female, depending on the partner.[9] Sexism cannot exist on Gethen, because everyone can become a woman. Le Guin simplifies the feminist utopia by removing sex as a fixed, immutable category. As a result, Winter is more believable as a country, despite the physical improbability of literal human androgyny. Because of the science fiction trope of an association of planets, Genly Ai need not be exiled from Winter, as Lane and Gilman must exile their narrators. Instead, the world peopled by beings of indeterminate sex becomes a part of the larger community of planets, and thereby directly challenges humanity's sex-based assumptions.

Like earlier feminist writers, Le Guin draws on the Demeter myth to create her utopia. The first explorer speculates about the origins of Winter and its unique ambisexuality and concludes that the ancient Hainish Empire created this people in an effort to eliminate war. Evoking the Demeter myth, the investigator discovers that the Gethenians were created during "a major interglacial" (89). However, the Hainish withdrew, leaving the ambisexual colonists on their own. The separation was accompanied by a return of the ice age to Winter in an origin myth that parallels that of Demeter and Persephone. The planet's harsh climate reflects their isolation from the ancient Hainish Empire and the more recent association of humans known as the Ekumen. Magical power to foretell the future reminds the reader and the envoy of the Gethenians' godlike origins.

As in other feminist utopias, in *The Left Hand of Darkness* the Demeter myth and mothering appear through allusions to specific elements from *Frankenstein*. Lord Estraven, Genly Ai's friend, is Frankenstein's monster re-created. His relationship with Genly replicates the ambivalence of Frankenstein's tie to his creation. Like Victor Frankenstein, Genly is codedly female (although to him, Estraven the alien seems feminine; in science fiction, the Other always represents the feminine). The Gethenians treat him "as if he were pregnant" (117). Through his narrative, Genly "creates" Estraven; it is Genly's offer of membership in the Ekumen that gives Estraven the chance to become his world's redeemer, and Genly's as well. Genly and Estraven are involved in a complicated love/hate relationship that culminates in a journey over the ice and snow of Winter.

Genly's following Estraven, first to Orgoyen and then on the Ice Crossing, parallels Frankenstein's pursuit of his creation. Like Frankenstein's monster, Estraven has incredible powers; he puts himself into a trance and travels many miles in snow without food or drink. Finally, isolated between the two kingdoms in an Arctic landscape, Genly and Estraven discover that, despite their alienness, "We are equals at last" (232). Shortly after this realization, Lord Estraven dies and leaves Genly Ai to mourn him—actions that follow the plot of *Frankenstein*. By understanding and loving Estraven, Genly discovers the feminine side of himself. He is transformed through this journey from an explorer-scientist into a writer-storyteller. In its positivism and embrace of the feminine, *Left Hand* differs from *Frankenstein*. Where Victor Frankenstein dies rather than accept his feminine side, Estraven dies so that Genly, the masculine figure, can accept and integrate his feminine side. This dramatic revision shows how feminist science fiction builds on, but drastically alters, the parameters of Shelley's novel.

Similarly, in *The Kin of Ata Are Waiting for You,* Bryant draws a portrait of a man learning to discover and accept the feminine side of himself. In a mythic pattern that prepares for Lessing's use of Demeter in the Canopus in Argos series, Ata functions as a Demeter to the patriarchal society of Earth, sending missionaries to protect and revitalize humanity. The Kin's nurturing function is symbolized by the narrator's regeneration. He was a murderer, rich and famous from the sexually violent spy thrillers he wrote. In Ata, he is completely transformed; his rebirth is symbolized by the daughter he creates and his understanding of a new way of superior parenting demonstrated by the Kin's emphasis on collectivity. "During the whole time I was there I never heard a baby cry," he comments (19). In the beginning, he is "confused because of the total lack of sexual roles" (19), but he grows to accept and understand human equality. He hopes his lover will be "a seer, a prophet" (187). The narrator returns to Earth and confesses his crime—and writes a book to tell all humans that "the Kin of Ata are waiting for you" (220). This is a beneficent version of Bulwer-Lytton's warning in *The Coming Race;* Bryant also prepares for Lessing's similarly positive message of a benevolent maternal empire in the Canopus in Argos series.

Like other feminist utopias, *The Kin of Ata Are Waiting for You* emphasizes relationships and community. Unlike the racist communities created by Lane and Gilman, the Kin of Ata are heterogeneous. Humans come to Ata from all over the Earth. The Kin's powers are communal; they heal the sick by chanting in a circle around the injured person, and they dance together as a tribe. The Kin's worship of the Sun appears primitive to the narrator, until he understands that this adulation is another manifestation of their desire for unity. The Kin freely enter one another's dreams and have no individual property. They even share the labor pains of women who give birth; consequently, any baby belongs to all the Kin. This emphasis on community in its purest form is an element of all feminist utopias, suggesting that from sharing comes strength.

The depiction of successful communities indirectly exposes capitalism's negative effects on women. To truly liberate women, Bryant says, the idea of property must be abandoned. Through the male narrator, Bryant directly links the concept of property with sexism. This narrator, an unwilling male explorer, kills a woman who was his possessive lover. He flees and, after an automobile accident, wakes up in Ata. Before he converts to the Kin, the narrator repeats the mistakes of Earth. He falls in love with Augustine, one of the Kin, and rapes her. Later, he kills one of the Kin whom he mistakenly believes is challenging him. Sickened by his own violence and possessiveness, the narrator confesses his sins to the Kin and is absolved. He has learned that humans cannot possess other beings, a lesson he demonstrates when he accepts that "his" daughter doesn't belong to him but is a part of all the Kin. His conversion suggests that, in the right circumstances, even the most hardened male chauvinist can be converted to feminine values.

While Russ, in *The Female Man,* is also interested in the interaction between the feminist utopia and what exists outside it, she threatens rather than implores as Le Guin and Bryant do. For this reason among others, Sarah Lefanu claims that "Joanna Russ is the single most important woman writer of science fiction" (173), an assessment borne out by an extended discussion of the text. The oxymoronic title of Russ's novel points to her assertive stance. Her narrator speaks in a Cassandra-like voice, and her female aliens will destroy men and enjoy it, as do Bulwer-Lytton's aliens in *The Coming Race.* Joanna, one of the main characters in Russ's novel, warns men, "Now I say *move over*" (140) and sends out her "daughter-book" (213) to tell what will happen if they do not listen. Russ threatens men with extinction if they do not accept women as equals, a reversal of the female dystopia, whose writers threaten men with extinction if they do not suppress women. *The Female Man* makes the most aggressive and powerful use of the female alien and the feminist utopia. The benefits of equality are only part of the message of Russ's multilayered novel. As Lefanu notes, "*The Female Man* breaks all rules of narrative fiction" (186). By doing so it forces us to reexamine and rethink the range of feminine stereotypes.[10]

The four female characters in *The Female Man* are Joanna, the writer, who through her art challenges male authority; Jeannie, a librarian and a quiet woman who knows that she deserves something better than the life of oppressed wife and mother, which her culture offers her in a parallel Earth that did not experience World War II; Janet, a strong, fearless, and intelligent woman from Whileaway, an Earth that has survived without men for centuries; and Jael, an Amazon from an Earth where men and women live separately and are at war. Only Janet and Jael are truly alien: Janet and the other female inhabitants of Whileaway reproduce and thrive without men, and Jael is physically alien—an artificially enhanced warrior with claws and metal teeth.[11] Through the concept of the female man—the alienated woman—Russ draws all four characters together to represent the murdered and dismembered female creature in *Frankenstein*. Through her characters, she evokes the Sphinx, the Medusa, and the witch, with their magical powers of reproduction and their separate cultures.

Alternative science shapes and makes possible these formidable female communities. Russ's female characters believe in magic, in feminine powers: "Men—in spite of everything—have no contact with or understanding of the insides of things. That's a realm that's denied them. Women's magic, women's intuition rules here" (108). This feminine intuition enables Whileaway to develop time travel. Perhaps because her culture wages war against men, Jael has the greatest feminine powers; she is called a "vampire" (163) and "faery" (188), and she scornfully describes male fears of "magic, childbirth, menstruation, witches" (189). Ironically, Jael herself is justification for these fears, because it is through these attributes that women threaten male dominance.

Like other feminist utopian writers, Russ evokes the Demeter myth. For the female man, mothering is problematic, full of separation and longing. One Whileaway story in particular symbolizes the separation experienced by all four women as they search for love. A daughter loses her mother in a natural catastrophe and is raised by bears, but she spends years looking for and eventually finds her mother. The emphasis on Persephone's activity rids the story of the embedded notion of women as passive beings, as victims, and the blissful reunion of the mother and daughter eradicates the idea that women must remain alienated from each other, as Demeter and Persephone are separated for part of every year. Lest the reader miss the point that the story applies to all women, Janet comments, "It was, of course, about me" (99). Mother/daughter separation and rediscovery are emphasized through winter, the symbol of Demeter's anguish at being separated from Persephone. Snow surrounds Laura, a young girl, and Janet as they struggle with their love for each other. Laura is frustrated by the demands of patriarchy; she is sent to a psychiatrist because she rejects the idea that "there is a mystical fulfillment in marriage and children" (65). She is "perpetually snowed in" (61) by the limited roles for women. Snow swirls around the house until Janet and Laura break through the defenses erected by Earth culture and make love. Here Russ depicts women's ability to dispense with men as lovers as well as fathers. Janet's concern saves Laura, her metaphoric daughter, from the ravages of the underworld of patriarchy. In this version of the myth, the mother and the daughter can provide each other with a love that protects and sustains them from the hostility of patriarchal society.

In *The Female Man,* strength comes from the expression of love from woman to woman, mother to daughter, lover to lover. The unification is represented by the Whileaway statue of God, "an outsized female figure as awful as Zeus" (103). This mysterious God is integral to Whileaway celebrations of the summer solstice, flowering of trees, bushes, planting of seeds and birth (102). When all four women meet for the first time, they experience "the kind of mother-love whose lack gets into your very bones" (158). As Lefanu argues, in *The Female Man,* "author, text and readers move around the paradigm of mother and child in a complex and at times contradictory way" (178).

Because Russ draws on the possibilities of feminist utopias, she is able to imagine cultures in which men and women live apart, or are literally at war, and thus can criticize our society. Rachel Blau DuPlessis's otherwise insightful article entitled "The Feminist Apologues of Lessing, Piercy and Russ" misses the central point of utopian science fiction by dismissing Russ's use of its tropes: "But for me, the sci-fi material, written as if on Russ' dare to herself, is presented to dress up. . . . It is not a future place nor future time, but is, instead, a mental place in the present" (6). In reducing utopian patterns to "sci-fi" dressing, DuPlessis ignores Russ's own history of commitment to the genre and the feminist co-option of utopias. *Only* in a feminist utopia can Whileaway be both a future place and a mental place in the present. The utopian tropes enable Russ to create an independent and autonomous Whileaway.

Charnas's *Motherlines* (1978) carries on the tradition of anger and threat articulated in *The Female Man.* The correspondence between Charnas's novels and Russ's is understandable, for appended to both *Walk to the End of the World,* the predecessor to *Motherlines,* and that novel is the following: " 'For too long science fiction has been dominated by masculine/sexist writing, but in recent years a group of women writers has been bringing new life and maturity into the field. These women are explicit and committed feminists. We're proud to be among them.' Joanna Russ / Suzy McKee Charnas" (*Motherlines* is also dedicated to "J.R.").

Charnas sets *Motherlines* in a postapocalyptic Earth to emphasize male mismanagement that has destroyed the Earth through nuclear catastrophe: "It was the combination of their [male] cleverness and stupidity that caused the Wasting" (60). Only a few men survive in Holdfast, a place of chaos and disaster in which all women are slaves. At the end of the book, all men are presumed dead, as lack of resources and the winter set in. Charnas too presents the men with the costs of patriarchy—eventual extinction. In contrast, the Riding Women and Free Fems, the two tribes of women, lead a utopian existence in the scorched desert.[12] As Marleen Barr explains, *Motherlines* "exemplif[ies] the notions of French feminist critic Hélène Cixous" (63), especially her emphasis on finding freedom through alternatives to patriarchal structures.

Charnas emphasizes alternative science through the eyes of a pregnant escaped slave. Exhausted from an arduous journey, Alldera is placed in a healing sleep by the Riding Women, who save both mother and child. "What magic did you do to save me?" (28), Alldera asks. The Mares, as they are also called, have many witchlike powers: they can tell the sex of the slave's unborn child, their speech is especially musical, and they have power over their horses, "a kind of magic" (53). All the Riding Women are descendants of women who were part of war experiments to channel the powers of the mind, or "witchery" (59). Women were used, one of the Mares explains, "because more of them had traces of the powers" (59); and to intensify their magic, the women were bred through trait doubling. Their daughters trick the men into leaving the lab, free the animals, and figure out how to continue parthenogenesis without the lab equipment. Alldera, the rescued slave, calls these women "great witches" (61), because instead of machines, the women use their horses to start their reproductive process, the motherlines of the title. Alternative science makes this utopia and its genetic continuance possible.

In this novel, Charnas similarly revises the Demeter myth, which shapes the plot of *Motherlines* and emphasizes a new feminist way of mothering. Bartkowski comments that "Charnas works at healing the mother-amazon split" (94) diagnosed in Gilman's *Herland*. Charnas does so by using Shelley's notion of alternative reproduction, but like Russ, she depicts this new species developing affective ties with its parents. Alldera intially rejects her lover, her daughter, and the Riding Women, but she returns to them when her daughter is initiated. The novel concludes with Alldera realizing that her daughter "was not the only one whose world had been gladdened with kindred, nor the only one to find and lose the mother of her heart" (246). Alldera and the Mares have solved the problems of artificially creating and

raising children by sharing the burden; no one person has the awesome responsibility of raising a child. Like Le Guin and Bryant, Charnas creates a
world in which reproduction is highly valued. Alldera is made a member of
the Riding Women because she can offer them a new motherline. In exchange, Alldera finds a mother's paradise. Her labor is made much easier
for her than it had been in Holdfast, and her child has a number of share-
mothers, who all breastfeed her. When Alldera becomes ill, she too is breast-
fed by the woman who later becomes her lover. As in *The Female Man*,
women's unity with a symbolic mother is valorized. Alldera thinks: "Imagine, being so easy and happy with a grown woman who had suckled you and
with whom your relations stretched back your entire life! It was wonderful
to bask on the edge of ease the women had with each other, the rich connectedness" (49). As with the Kin of Ata, the Mares share everything, including sex and mothering.

Neither completely inclusionary nor exclusionary, Marge Piercy's *Woman on the Edge of Time* (1976) provides an example of an intermediate
stance for the feminist utopia. The "woman on the edge of time" visits the
utopia and the dystopia, enabling the reader to compare both to twentieth-
century Earth. In the feminist utopia, humans are almost ambisexual; Connie, the protagonist, cannot tell the difference between the men and the
women, in part because they have "reformed pronouns" (42) to reflect male
and female equality. In this future, men as well as women breastfeed children. Neither bears children, but instead they practice exogenesis and can
travel through time using only their minds. Their powers are reflected in
earlier times in the receptivity of women. Only women are aware of the time
travelers, and, as Luciente, the woman from the future, informs Connie,
"Most we've reached are females and many of those in mental hospitals and
prisons" (196). Piercy prepares us for Lessing's Canopus Empire, whose
agents are also women wrongly condemned as insane. In feminist science
fiction, the imprisonment of Connie and women like her exposes the inability of patriarchal society to listen to the outsider.

Piercy directly criticizes dystopias by including them in her science fiction. When Connie travels to Mattapoisett, she discovers a feminist paradise
where everyone has a room of her own and there is no racism or sex discrimination. The utopia is at war with a male dystopia, which Connie briefly
visits by accident. There, women are treated as property, enslaved by technology that traps them in cells with drugs and pornographic television. One
of the "sense-all" movies repeats the plot and slogans of misogynistic female dystopias: "'When Fems Flung to Be Men': In Age of Uprisings, two
fem libbers meet in battle. . . . SD man zaps in, fights both" (293). This dys-

topia is an extrapolation of the mental hospital that Connie inhabits, while the utopia demonstrates socialist-feminist principles put into action.

Connie herself holds the key to the two possible futures—female dystopia or feminist utopia—emphasizing the importance of women to the future. She practices magic, as do her appropriately named friend Sybil and all women in the future. Connie is both a "sender" and "catcher" of time travelers' telepathy. She is called a witch on several occasions, and there are numerous examples of her magic, including her ability to tell instantly when her niece is pregnant and to foresee the immediate future. Her gifts and her resistance to patriarchy result in her incarceration, as it does for other women, including her friend Sybil.

In the future, these magical powers are nurtured into a soft science. "It was part of women's long revolution. When we were breaking all the old hierarchies" (105), says Luciente, a woman from the future. They share the powers of birth with men and hone skills of telepathy and precognition and heal with their minds and talk to animals. What seems insane or diabolical in the twentieth century becomes a science in the twenty-first. Luciente, the time traveler, is first and foremost "a scientist" (274). The emphasis on science in feminist utopias legitimates women. It is on this basis that feminist utopian writers build their plots, which focus on community and relationships between men and women. As it is in other female utopias, soft science is explicitly contrasted to the negative hard science exemplified by Connie's mistreatment by the doctors who will not hear her message. The doctors are described as "cold, calculating, ambitious, believing themselves rational and superior," and they are condemned for "chasing the crouching female through the brain with a scalpel" (282). As Bartkowski explains, "That Connie is a Chicana single mother makes her words even more susceptible to remaining unheard and denied at Bellevue Hospital, a state institution administered by white, professional heterosexists!" (62). Piercy completes the dissection of male science through Connie's retelling of the true story of male doctors playing with female lives through placebo birth control substitutes. Like Lessing's *Four-Gated City* and *Briefing for a Descent into Hell,* Piercy's *Woman on the Edge of Time* interweaves scientific reports with Connie's story to shock and alienate the reader from hard science.

In *Woman on the Edge of Time,* as in other feminist utopias, science and mothering are interrelated rather than antithetical. In one possible future, humans share mothering responsibilities so that each child has three co-mothers. Connie has been dismissed as a child abuser by the social workers, and her child is taken away from her. In the feminist utopia, however, she realizes her potential by becoming a co-mother. Even more important, she discovers her lost child in another character, Dawn, whom she can now love and nurture. Through snow imagery, Piercy recalls the myth of Demeter and her forced separation from her daughter. Connie has been torn from her child by the court psychiatrist, who has declared her unfit to mother—the male doctor acts the role of the God of the Underworld and seduces her daughter with the wealth of an adoptive family. As Connie thinks about her daughter in her brother's greenhouse, it begins to snow. As she bid the people of the feminist utopia good-bye, "Big disks of snow came tilting and turning down where already several inches lay thick, rounding all corners and softening straight lines, an expanse of white across the square marked only by the tracks of children playing" (370). Connie's last vision of the image of her daughter in the future is of her covered with snowflakes. Piercy repeats the Demeter myth to show the sacrifices women make for their daughters in a patriarchy. Like Gilman and Lane, Piercy asserts through Connie's rediscovered mothering that feminists make better mothers. In our fallen world, sexism and racism corrupt Connie and take her child away so that she does not have a chance to be a good mother.

Luciente tells Connie that she will help to decide which of the two possible futures happen, the feminist utopia or the misogynistic hell. Through Luciente's plea for help, Piercy reminds her readers that we hold the future in our hands and that only we can protect the Connies of the world and take steps to ensure the existence of a positive future for women. This future will exist only if women work together and stress community. As Luciente tells Connie, "we don't buy or sell anything" (64) and "we share the exciting jobs and the dull jobs" (123). Like Bryant's Kin of Ata, Piercy's utopians share dreams, birth, and death. Racism does not exist in their world because their genes are deliberately mixed. Like Charnas's Mares, the humans of the future lead an ecologically sound existence and are close to nature, even to communicating mentally with animals. This is a pattern in feminist utopias identified by Albinski, who explains that women's identification with nature becomes "liberating because it is depicted positively" (*Women's Utopias* 163–64).

Unlike mainstream novels, science fiction retains and revitalizes powerful female communities that thrive without men. Bulent Somay's description of "a high-water mark [in utopian fiction] impossible to maintain after the ebbing of the radical wave of the 1960's and early 70's" (36) does not take into account the power of feminism and the vigor of the feminist utopia. As Daphne Patai asserts, "Feminism, today, is the most utopian project around" (151). And feminist utopianism continues to flourish in novels like

Suzette Haden Elgin's *Native Tongue* and *The Judas Rose,* in which the author, trained as a linguist, creates a women's language. Like Marion Zimmer Bradley's Darkover series, Elgin's work defies conventional literary boundaries, for she offers copies of a grammar and dictionary to the women's language in the first pages of the novel. Sheri Tepper's *Gate to Women's Country* (1989) manifests the reversal inherent in the feminist utopia; in her female-run world, men are bred by women. Both Elgin's and Tepper's texts use the feminist utopia to explore ways that women could develop to change men. The publication of Tepper's novel as a mass market fiction rather than exclusively science fiction suggests how well established and acceptable this tradition has become, at least to publishers.

How successful utopianism is as a cultural strategy remains to be seen. As defined in this study, feminist utopias attempt to leave the real world behind, and they rely on rupture and separation.[13] Nevertheless, the reader of feminist utopias must constantly question the degree of displacement they achieve. Even as the writers imagine a matriarchal or all-female ideal world, they do so in response to, and from the inside of, patriarchal culture. One evidence of this limitation is the racism of the early feminist utopias; another sign is the slippage toward simple role reversal in which women use men in the same ways women have been oppressed by men. It may be that the violence lurking beneath the surface of many feminist utopias indicates the frustration of women trapped in the hostile world of patriarchal culture, and hence is understandable if not entirely defensible.

Feminist science fiction, however, rejects the essentialism and simplicity of the feminist utopian strategy. As I discuss in detail in the next chapter, feminist science fiction incorporates the strategy of utopia but always includes the possibility of men and women successfully integrating in a nonsexist, nonracist, nonclassist society. Rather than attempt to step outside the patriarchy, these books hold out the promise of an internal coup to the benefit of men and women. Feminist science fiction exists in a dialogue with female utopias. It rejects the underlying separatist premise of the female utopia and suggests alternatives to isolationism.[14]

Notes

1. While utopians consider science fiction a genre of utopia, I place it here as a subset of science fiction.

2. Pearson notes (55–57) the importance of home but neglects to emphasize its

radical transformation in feminist science fiction. Home becomes the mother/ daughter relationship of female lovers.

3. Lane's book has been described as the "undeservedly obscure precursor of . . . feminist utopias" (Segal 67).

4. Albinski notes that "Mizorans" is "an incomplete anagram of Amazons" (*Women's Utopias* 49).

5. The feminist utopia declines to enter this competition. Like the feminist explorers of Le Guin's "Sur," who reach the North Pole but decline to trumpet their achievements or proclaim themselves "first," feminist utopias rely on the Arctic for protection and a quiet demonstration of the ability to thrive where men cannot go.

6. See, for example, the discussion of Victorian utopias in Albinski, "'The Laws of Justice, of Nature, and of Right': Victorian Feminist Utopias." Jean Pfaelzer discusses the ideology of separatism and essentialism that undergirds *Mizora* and Gilman's reification of gender differences (147, 151). Bartkowski criticizes Gilman for her essentialism (*Feminist Utopias* 27).

7. Unfortunately, Schmitz is the only male who has written a feminist utopia. Theodore Sturgeon's *Venus Plus X* is not a female utopia because, as Scott Sanders notes in "Woman as Nature in Science Fiction," *Venus Plus X* "places the blame for oppressive social conditions on the biologically innate temperament of the sexes" (72).

8. Most critics focus on Le Guin's *Dispossessed* to discuss the utopian aspects of her novels. However, Winter has also been discussed as a utopia by Jewel P. Rhodes, in "Ursula K. Le Guin's *The Left Hand of Darkness:* Androgyny and the Feminist Utopian Vision."

9. Gethenians who wish to remain one sex or the other are considered perverted, but they are not lesbians or homosexuals. Le Guin doesn't address the issue of sexual preference in Western terms.

10. As discussed in the last chapter, Russ also looks forward to postmodern feminist science fiction. Chronologically, *The Female Man* belongs to this group of female utopias, but it should also be seen as a forerunner of 1980s feminist science fiction.

11. DuPlessis notes the significance of Jael's name: she is "the neo-Biblical nailer" (2, 7).

12. In her feminist utopia, Charnas shows that science fiction can be used to write exclusively about women's relationships, a new development for the genre. Because of her literary skill, Charnas has been acclaimed by Barr as "an important contributor to feminist utopian . . . science fiction." Barr claims too that, "as Charnas herself has been changed by writing, her readers also have the potential to make changes in their own lives" (47)—a claim supported by Patai's research in utopian fiction.

13. Since I discuss utopias as a narrative strategy, the marketing of the texts as science fiction rather than utopias is of less importance than their structure. In my reading, utopias are a subcategory of science fiction.

14. Here I agree with Bartkowski, who says: "One of the keynotes of feminist utopias [the texts she discusses, which I consider feminist science fiction] as distinct from earlier ones is the inclusion of alternate futures, 'wrong,' 'false,' atavistic futures which signal the possibility of nightmarish backlash to the 'fact' of women's liberation" (61).

FOUR

Feminist Science Fiction

While the feminist utopia can provide an effective setting in which patriarchal science can be criticized, the utopia's assertion of difference cannot suffice as a critique by itself because it is limited by its separatist demarcation. Separatism enables societies that completely reject sexism and patriarchy, but these societies are finally unsatisfactory because they rely on the eradication of men through plague or war. Although their strategies differ, feminist science fiction and feminist utopias complement rather than contradict each other, and feminist science fiction frequently contains feminist utopian societies—for example, Zone Three in Lessing's *Marriages between Zones Three, Four, and Five*. Because feminist science fiction and feminist utopias offer different messages, the same writer may choose to write both, as did Le Guin in *The Left Hand of Darkness* (a feminist utopia) and in *Rocannon's World* and *Always Coming Home* (both science fiction).[1]

Of the two strategies identified by Derrida, to attack from within or to affirm absolute rupture and difference, the first distinguishes feminist science fiction from the feminist utopia. Feminist science fiction repeats what is implicit in the founding concepts of patriarchal society, the dichotomy between masculine and feminine that traditionally oppresses women but which feminist science fiction uses to empower itself. Feminist science fiction looks at the dualities of masculine and feminine, traditional science and feminist science, and shifts the terms of the pairing to privilege the marginal over what is usually central. And in the process it deconstructs the binarisms of patriarchy.

Feminist science fiction depicts individual women as more powerful than their feminist utopian counterparts and stresses character development to a greater degree than do feminist utopias, which tend to emphasize community. Feminist science fiction has more room for ambiguity and difference than the utopias do, and such diversity reflects the shift within feminism itself from Feminism to feminisms or from women's rights to issues of gender, race, and class. While feminist utopias do not oversimplify, they do isolate issues of gender and frequently, especially in the early utopias, espouse a model of essentialism. Feminist utopias resolutely idealize all-female societies, while feminist science fiction depicts conflicts between opposing points of view. To appreciate the change in feminist writings, feminist science fiction should be read in the context of feminist utopias and male-dominated science fiction, for these are the texts to which feminist science fiction reacts.

Unlike a feminist utopia, which is usually sexually segregated, a feminist science fiction novel is integrated sexually and, frequently, racially: consider, for example, McIntyre's *Starfarers,* Sheri Tepper's *Gate to Women's Country,* and Butler's *Mind of My Mind.*[2] While the feminist utopia is separated and isolated geographically, as it is in Gilman's *Herland,* or in time, as it is in Russ's *Female Man* and Piercy's *Woman on the Edge of Time,* a feminist science fiction novel often occurs in the near future or in a world that closely resembles Earth culturally and geographically, as does the world in Tiptree's *Up the Walls of the World.* A feminist science fiction novel focuses not only on female autonomy, as *The Female Man* does, but also, in texts like Vinge's *Snow Queen* or Norton's Witch World series, on how an egalitarian society can be achieved. In feminist science fiction, female writers show how mental powers and art benefit men and women. Without rejecting the achievements of male-dominated technology, feminist science fiction writers suggest that the harnessing of mental powers has more to offer the human race than hard science alone. This feminist exploration of the unknown pushes science fiction beyond its old limitations of depending on technology for plot and theme. Emphasizing the brain also allows women greater participation in science fiction, for the brain is presumably sexless.

Despite feminist science fiction's emphasis on the commonalities between men and women, the texts are informed by what has been identified by psychologists as a feminine sensibility. Like Carol Gilligan's female subjects, feminist science fiction writers valorize interdependence over independence and mercy over justice, values that are also used in the feminist utopia. However, the feminist utopia and feminist science fiction differ in the emphasis placed on these values. In the feminist utopia, these values structure the entire society, while in the feminist science fiction text they comprise one possible frame or one of a competing set of values. The differences between the feminist utopia and feminist science fiction rest on a fundamental distinction in emphasis: feminist science fiction stresses the benefits to men and women of sexual equality, and it usually does so through the particular relationships of male and female protagonists.

Feminist science fiction draws together the disparate threads of the female dystopia, the male-dominated tradition of science fiction, and the feminist utopia, weaving these into a new science fiction tradition that challenge the genre's misogynistic bias by subverting science fiction tropes. Norton, Butler, and Vinge are a few of the popular science fiction writers who depict women wielding magical powers and defeating male-dominated technology. Their female characters are powerful *and* sympathetic female aliens and rulers. In feminist science fiction, the triumph of the female alien is the triumph of a feminist vision of the world. It is also the victory of soft science over hard science—but always in worlds in which men can participate.

Contemporary woman writers use the tropes of science fiction to depict worlds that are nonsexist, nonhierarchical, and centered on androgynous values shaped by feminist concerns. Through the "mythology of the modern world," as Le Guin describes science fiction, woman science fiction writers rewrite old myths that inscribe women. Like Hélène Cixous, feminist science fiction writers hear the laugh of the Medusa and transform misogynist myths of horrific female power into empowering portrayals of feminine strength. The figures of the Sphinx, the Medusa, and the witch are reborn as heroines in feminist science fiction. Using myth and the tropes of science fiction, woman writers create two versions of the revised fairy tales feminist critics ask for.[3] First, feminist science fiction writers deconstruct the binaries of masculine and feminine science through the reclamation of magic and art as alternative sciences and the construction of societies altered by such practices. Second, using material from traditional science fiction, feminist science fiction writers revise misogynistic myths about female power—the story of Demeter and Persephone and a more recent version, the fairy tale of the Snow Queen. Through the creation of successful Demeters and Persephones and the setting of apocalypse evoked by the Earth goddess's wrath at being separated from her daughter, feminist science fiction uses the stories of patriarchal society to deconstruct it.

Masculine Science versus Feminine Magic

■ This new feminist tradition strengthens what has traditionally been the weak term in a binary opposition to finally overcome the dichotomy. The opposition between male-dominated science and feminine magic is exposed, only to be deconstructed. Because male-dominated science is identified as hard and feminine magic as soft and unscientific, this opposition also appears as science versus art. Witches turn out to be scientific and men turn out to be feminine (or at least to have the capacity to be so). Often the plot of a feminist novel focuses on a war in which one side is male-dominated and conventionally scientific, while the other is headed by women and powered by alternative science. Women writers present alternative science as overcoming and then incorporating the forces of traditional technology. As Russ explains, "There's no consensual way of talking about what makes up the daily lives of most women, so it's not surprising that women [science fiction writers] have been exploring telepathy, ESP, magic" (qtd. in McCaffery 207). Those feminine qualities that male-dominated science fiction writers describe as liabilities develop into empowering tools in feminist science fiction. In a reversal of the tropes of traditional science fiction, male characters adopt the values of the feminist utopias.[4]

This feminist science fiction tradition predates feminist criticism, but, ironically, critics are only beginning to appreciate the woman-centered message of writers like Norton, one of science fiction's most prolific and popular authors.[5] In the early 1960s, while male writers like Isaac Asimov were still writing about the stereotypical old maid, Norton was expanding the parameters of science fiction with her strong female protagonists and playing with the dichotomies that permeate feminist science fiction. She depicts successful female witches who rule through their magic, and her novels posit an alternative to technology, namely, psionics. As it is in mainstream science fiction, psionics is here particularly associated with women. Unlike science fiction by male writers, Norton's fiction valorizes feminine values and female rulers and forces the reader to examine accepted ideas about science and progress. Her Estcarp witches, for example, implicitly suggest a reevaluation of Western civilization's treatment of witches. By depicting an alternate world in which magic and witchcraft are powerful and venerated, Norton shows what our culture lost when it persecuted witches. She also emphasizes the idea of feminine science or magic as a power potentially available to men as well as women and does so through symbols like jewelry that are usually associated with art rather than science. By having gems as technology, Norton confounds and confuses customary distinctions between science and art, forcing readers to question their assumptions about each category.

Especially because she has been neglected by critics, Norton deserves our attention, for she was the first and is perhaps the most influential feminist science fiction author. The patterns she has created appear throughout feminist science fiction. Since the 1930s, she has turned out dozens of science fiction novels, a number of them part of a series, and many women writers acknowledge the effect of her work.[6] Vinge's novel *Psion* (1982) is dedicated to Norton, whom she describes as the main character's "spiritual godmother." The prolific and Hugo Award–winning C. J. Cherryh claims, "A lot of us who create worlds, whether we write them or dream them secretly, owe a great deal to [Norton's Witch World]" (*Lore* 8), and she praises Norton for being the first writer to create active female characters (9). Norton reverses the pattern of the male savior from the female dystopia; instead, her male explorers follow female rulers and learn to practice alternative science, or psionics. This conversion usually occurs in the context of a cultural conflict between matriarchal and patriarchal cultures. Feminine magic, such as the ability to communicate telepathically, are placed in literal and metaphorical conflict with male-dominated science, which relies exclusively on machines. This paradigm is first and most clearly delineated in Norton's Witch World series.[7]

In the Witch World series, male explorers convert to feminine values during a cultural conflict between a matriarchal society ruled by witches who work closely with Nature and a male-identified society run by a cyborg, a man who is part machine. Here *Witch World* differs from most feminist utopias in which such conflicts have already been resolved in favor of the feminist societies.[8] The reader is clearly meant to identify with the witches because their characters are sympathetically depicted. At the same time, the novel's protagonist is a man, Simon Tregarth, who stumbles into this world and who adopts the witches' values and accepts their science. While he joins their world, however, he also teaches the witches about the importance of gender equality.

Tregarth is first taught to respect the powers of Nature, so clearly allied to women. In feminist science fiction, female closeness to Nature becomes a powerful science. Using their psionic powers to draw on Nature's fury, the Estcarp witches work together and with Nature to defeat their enemy. As one of the witches explains, they are able to use the sea as a weapon because "we have a portion of the sea in our veins" (54). The people of Estcarp all have a "queer affinity with the land itself and with the beasts and birds" (208). The witches' victory suggests that women's minds working with Nature can defeat the mechanically dominated patriarchy. Through the cooperation symbolized by the characters' joining hands, Norton implies that feminism can defeat the overwhelming forces of patriarchy. At the same time, the witches' triumph emphasizes that a feminist culture offers an alternative for women *and* men. Through Tregarth's conversion to the witches' cause, Norton exposes the closed-mindedness of Western culture and science. Unless man can rid himself of superstition and sexism, as Tregarth does, he will never discover the psionic powers of the mind.

Tregarth's conversion depicts the possibility and benefits of men adopting the values of alternate science. This embittered soldier finds a home, companions, and a world to which he can devote himself. Unlike real-life science, alternative science is open to both sexes in feminist science fiction. Unlike the women in the feminist utopias, Norton's witches do not use their powers to exclude men. Instead, Tregarth's acceptance of his wife and the witches leads to magic powers for men and women—both their male and female children have mental powers, breaking the single-sex domination of Estcarp. This demonstration of alternate science's power shows the male reader the importance and benefits of sharing power with women.

The witches' success over their enemies also evokes the power of women's anger and suggests the dangers of suppressing women. Through one witch named Jaelithe, Norton evokes the biblical woman who killed the general who was oppressing her people. Russ draws on the same mythical heroine through the character Jael in *The Female Man,* but in Norton's feminist science fiction, Jaelithe is more flexible. Jaelithe retains her powers after marriage and converts a soldier (Tregarth) to the witches' cause. Although feminist science fiction endorses the values of feminist utopias, it also stresses cooperation between the sexes. However, Norton and other feminist science fiction writers use their novels to suggest that if men do not share their power, women will use psionics to wrest control from them. Because this science involves nature, trances, and physical contact, psionics seems more an art than the mechanically based rational science practiced primarily by men. Psionics symbolizes the power of feminist art to persuade and convert and makes male and female equality seem possible and attractive. Feminist science fiction thus simultaneously cajoles and threatens the male reader.

Norton also comments in *Witch World* on the sexism of present-day Earth. For example, the Estcarp witches mistakenly believe that only virgin women can practice psionics, and Norton uses the witches' sexist belief to expose the hideousness of rape and of women replicating sexist standards. In the Witch World series, men rape the witches to rob them of their powers, showing how men use rape to intimidate and threaten women. By including a rape survivor in the story, Norton shows how devastating the effects of rape can be. This depiction of rape as a means of intimidating and controlling women is an early feminist analysis of the politics of rape, and its appearance emphasizes the importance of science fiction as a feminist arena.[9] Through fictional characters, Norton recasts the issue of rape to make explicit its function of oppressing women.

Past sexism can also be criticized through the possibilities of science fiction settings. The association of female aliens with witches gives Norton the opportunity to rewrite history. Her use of the witches as a separate society enables her to employ structural elements of the feminist utopia, but unlike the feminist utopia, Witch World also exposes the dangers of isolation and separatism. Its connectedness to other societies shows that Norton is also criticizing the limitations of utopian worlds. While the Estcarp witches are admirable, their powers are waning and the series as a whole looks toward the acquisition of witchlike powers by both men and women. First, though, Norton uses science fiction to show witches triumphing over mechanically based technology. Setting Estcarp on an alternative world allows Norton to suggest what our world lost by persecuting and exterminating practitioners of alternative science. Furthermore, she uses Witch World to depict the possibility of men learning from women and becoming part of a society based on feminine values.

Vinge repeats Norton's patterns—and acknowledges her debt to Norton—in her Hugo Award–winning work. Her highly acclaimed and popular novel *The Snow Queen* follows the paradigm of feminine magic versus male-dominated science. In marked contrast to Norton's engaging but brief tales, Vinge's feminist message is embedded in a long, engrossing novel with likable, believable characters. For this reason, *The Snow Queen* is one of the most entrancing novels in the feminist tradition. Vinge's complex weaving of myth, fairy tale, and plot never flags as a story because she beguiles her readers as she polemicizes. She depicts the male/female struggle with a psychological depth missing in science fiction until recently. Yet, at the same time, the young lovers Moon and Sparks function on a symbolic level by epitomizing the choices that individuals and cultures make. Moon discovers the benefits of a matriarchal alternative science, while Sparks adopts and later rejects male-dominated science. By making her readers identify with Moon, Vinge subtly exposes sexism and posits an alternative mythology.

Vinge uses Moon, the heroine and a female alien, to show the benefits of being a cultural outsider. Moon is estranged from her culture's corrupt ruler, who is dominated by the off-world patriarchy, the Kharemough Hegemony, which depends on advanced technology remnants of an ancient empire but which denies the "natives" any access to their knowledge. The Hegemony exploits the natural resources of Tiamat,[10] Moon's world. The Hegemony's dependence on hard technology also has kept humanity in a postapocalyptic ignorance about the powers of the human mind. Sibyls, native priestesses who are able to see the future, are dismissed as superstitious fools by the Hegemony and banned from the cities of Tiamat. Because of its adherence to technology, the Hegemony unnecessarily exploits the life-giving fluid of an intelligent species, the mers. In this situation of human ignorance, in a universe that has lost the stupendous technology of the ancient empire, feminist skill triumphs. Only Moon and the other sibyls retain links to the power of the Old Empire, which practiced soft science by using human minds rather than machines to develop and store knowledge.

Just as Moon proves to be morally superior to the Hegemony, her psionics proves superior to the Hegemony's machine-based science. By the end of the novel, one of the Hegemony leaders admits, "'There's nothing I can do'" (370) to affect the Change, the isolation of the world from space travel because of the fluctuations of a black hole approaching Tiamat. Although the Hegemony has the most advanced mechanical technology, it cannot traverse the Black Gate, a revolving black hole that will cut off Tiamat from the rest of the universe. Using the powers of her mind, Moon succeeds where machines fail when she pulls a spaceship through the previously unnavigable black hole that keeps her planet isolated and powerless.[11] Alone, she breaks the stranglehold of the Hegemony, but hers is also the triumph of feminine psionics over mechanical science and of soft science over hard science.

In her world and in the tradition of woman science fiction writers, Moon represents the apex of practitioners of feminine magic. A feminist heroine who cares about both her male and female subjects, Moon will share her knowledge of the Old Empire's science. In contrast to the male-dominated Hegemony, which uses technology to enslave indigenous populations and to exploit their resources, Moon uses her sibylline powers, created by a female scientist to keep alive the Old Empire's knowledge, to transform her world. As the reference to the classical Sibyls suggests, Moon's heritage can be traced back to a source common to Shelley's *Last Man,* whose narrator is also called a sibyl. Moon is a futuristic witch, a beneficent version of the witches in the female dystopia and the male science fiction tradition.

Like Norton, Vinge draws on history for her depiction of the sibyls. They are witches who are even more powerful than Norton's Estcarpians, but, unlike Norton, Vinge provides an elaborate scientific justification for sibylline powers. The sibyls are infected with an artificially created disease that joins their minds to an immense computer from the Old Empire. This combination of magic, or mental sciences, with the hardware of a computer is typical of feminist science fiction's tendency toward a synthesis of female and male paradigms of science.[12] The scientific explanation of sibylline powers makes those powers appear plausible, just as Ehrenreich and English's *Witches, Midwives, Nurses* explains the science of witchcraft. Like real doctors, however, the male-dominated Hegemony refuses to explore this advanced technology. Out of fear, it bans sibyls from the capital city and dismisses sibylline power as superstition. Vinge's creation of the sibyls shows how foolish and shortsighted the male Hegemony and, by implication, Western culture are for outlawing alternative science.

The association of female scientists with witches, their struggle against a hostile and patriarchal empire, and the eventual vindication of female rule is a reversal of the misogynistic paradigms of the female dystopias and most mainstream science fiction up to the 1970s. But writers like Norton and Vinge have accomplished much more than a mere inversion. As the many honors bestowed on feminist writers attest, woman science fiction writers are also raising the standards of the genre. The feminist message is but one part of these complex and multilayered texts. Norton and Vinge and other women writers depict believable and sympathetic female characters, compelling even a potentially hostile audience of science fiction readers to care about women's issues. Here woman writers differ dramatically from the writers of the female dystopias and many mainstream science fiction writers. The reader cannot become involved with cardboard female characters like Asimov's Susan Calvin, who appears in his famous Robot collections *I, Robot,* and *The Rest of the Robots.* While feminist science fiction contains characters who change over time, male-dominated science fiction emphasizes how technology develops. Norton and Vinge make the reader empathize with their female scientists and their feminist goals,[13] a quality that shapes Tanith Lee's *Silver-Metal Lover,* Sydney J. Van Syoc's *Darkchild,* and Julian May's Saga of Pliocene Exile series, among many others.

One of the reasons that women make better rulers is their practice of psionics as an art as well as a science. Ironically, in the mainstream tradition, art has long been considered antithetical to utopias and to science fiction, as, for example, in the expulsion of art from Plato's *Republic* and its exclusion from science fiction (Ketterer 96). In feminist science fiction, art is not excluded but embraced. As Moon becomes the Summer Queen, she dons a beautiful mask, made for her by another sibyl, which expresses

Moon's values because it is both beautiful and functional. Like her mask, Moon will emphasize artistic *and* technological achievements. Her choice of art as symbol appears in the jeweled trefoil that marks all sibyls, just as Norton's witches each possess a gem that identifies their powers. Norton's association of jewelry with power, like her use of female accoutrements as an alternative to the guns of the Kolder, is a pattern that Lessing adopts in her science fiction series Canopus in Argos, where jewelry becomes a weapon. Lessing also adopts Norton's underlying feminist principles and their expression through psionics. This identification of art as power recurs too in Le Guin's "Sur," where female explorers in the Arctic create beautiful ice sculptures, proving through art rather than a phallic, nationalistic symbol like a flag that they were the first to reach the North Pole.

Woman characters in feminist science fiction novels use art to strengthen and record the effects of their psionic powers. The feminist emphasis on art intensifies the hard/soft science dichotomy as a gender-based conflict that distinguishes the power of female characters from male scientists. Feminist science fiction uses art to bridge this cultural dichotomy; female characters in feminist science fiction practice a combination of art and science or use science to create art. For example, in Anne McCaffrey's *Ship Who Sang,* Helva uses her computer capabilities to surpass all human artistic achievements by playing any part, or singing any role, perfectly. Her singing ability enables her to defeat a crazed dictator who captures her male partner, a hard scientist. While her male partners die or retire, Helva lives on to perform many other remarkable feats with her artistic powers. Similarly, Lee's Silver-Metal Lover uses her writing to record her telepathic experience with her robot lover and to defeat the technocrat society that separates her from the robot.

One feminist writer has made art and psionics the center of all her novels and, in an innovative twist, defines art as involving linguistic rather than plastic arts. Suzette Haden Elgin is a poet and former professor of linguistics whose two series, the Communipath novels and the popular Ozark Fantasy Trilogy, have attracted scholarly and popular attention. Throughout her science fiction novels, Elgin particularly demonstrates the importance of art for women, and her Communipath series crystallizes the feminist use of art in science fiction. The first of the novels, *The Communipaths,* is narrated by a young girl just beginning to develop her psionic powers. Her journal is equated in importance to her psionic powers (which can only reach people within a few miles) because the journal provides her with an even larger audience. In *Furthest,* Bess, the heroine, uses her capabilities as a mindwife to challenge the patriarchal culture that restricts such women to concubinage. Similarly, Jacinthe, a twelve-year-old girl in a male-dominated culture complete with harems, uses her poetic skill to obtain a ruling position in the highest profession of poet. On Abba, it is the poets who wage war with words. Jacinthe defeats a male poet, uses her linguistic skill to save ten colonies, and even heals through her command of words.

Art becomes the salvation of the female ruler and is the means by which she rules. The female rulers' use of art also emphasizes Elgin's and other feminist science fiction writers' co-option of science fiction itself. Like the female rulers they create, feminist science fiction writers use art to challenge male authority and revise patriarchal culture. Elgin's use of journals, letters, and reports as the basis for the narrative recalls *Frankenstein*'s codedly female audience. Walton's narrative is more powerful than Frankenstein's creation, who vanishes into the Arctic landscape. Without Walton's account, both creator and monster would be invisible, their story lost. So soft science, aided by writing, proves more durable than hard science.

Similarly, in feminist science fiction, women rulers raise art to the status and power of science. On Elgin's Furthest, women practice psionics, and their title, mindwife, is a title clearly meant to recall midwife, with its attendant association with magic and witchcraft. In *At the Seventh Level,* Jacinthe mentally heals with her poetry and uses her powers to communicate with the truly alien, animalistic Serpent People, recalling the witches's fabled power to communicate with animals. This association of witchlike power with artistic achievement is common in feminist science fiction and strengthens feminist claims to alternate science. Feminist science differs not only in effect but in approach. Women scientists use art to strengthen their powers and to present their message, to communicate, as Jacinthe does, with an alien species. In feminist science fiction, the aliens are likely to be men, but unlike male science fiction, these texts emphasize the importance of communicating with cross-gendered aliens.

Their female protagonists' use of art parallels the feminist subversion of science fiction. Like their authors, feminist characters use art to proselytize, and in this way, characters mimic the subversive strategy employed by their authors. Through the use of art, one of the patriarchal house's stones, feminist writers expose its frame. As Lessing does in her space fiction, women opt for nonmechanical weapons. Feminist tools are ideas and art, media that eventually prevail in feminist science fiction. The conflict between soft and hard science is resolved in favor of the female-identified soft science. Woman writers have embedded their own struggles in their writing, and the popular and critical success of their work vindicates their fictions.

The Snow Queen and Demeter

■ The Demeter paradigm intertwines with the other patterns described in this chapter, none of which are exclusive. In one novel, the alternate science angle might be stressed, but the book might still include references to the Demeter myth or art. This general crossover is part of the deconstructing of binarisms that is a defining quality of feminist science fiction. Just as central to the breakdown of categorization is the revision of myth that emphasizes the relations of women to women rather than focusing on woman as seen by man. As feminist science fiction writers emphasize relations among women, they revise traditional myths, especially that of Demeter and Persephone. Feminist revisions of science fiction, then, involve new mythmaking that focuses on traditionally female concerns such as familial relationships, mothering, and social cooperation. These writers create feminist fairy tales about worlds based on what are identified as feminine values that provide alternatives to patriarchal science and society. By connecting their science fiction to the Demeter myth, women writers can examine female power in a fallen—patriarchal—world and criticize mother/daughter relationships in a sexist culture.

In the Greek version of the myth, Demeter loses her only daughter, Persephone, to the Lord of the Underworld, who abducts Persephone and carries her off by force to his underground kingdom. In her anger and grief, Demeter refuses to attend to the Earth, which turns into a "frozen desert. The green and flowering land was icebound and lifeless because Persephone had disappeared" (Hamilton 49). This ancient myth is a version of the Fall, explaining why the Earth is no longer Edenic. Unlike the Christian version in which the hardships of the seasons are explained by Eve's sin and a patriarchal God's justice, this Greek legend explains that a goddess, a mother, purposely creates the seasons to show her anger.

Settings of ice and snow, like the winter Demeter brought about, appear with remarkable frequency in feminist science fiction and usually overtly recall this myth. Piercy's *Woman on the Edge of Time* and Russ's *Female Man,* both female utopias, and Vinge's *Snow Queen* contain such settings which evoke the myth on a number of levels varying from the literal to the metaphorical. In Lee's *Silver-Metal Lover,* the daughter, Jane, struggles to understand her remote and stratos-inhabiting mother, Demeta. In the Canopus in Argos series, Lessing's human characters struggle to reunite with their metaphorical mother, the empire Canopus. Similarly, the heroine of Norton's *Ordeal in Otherwhere* finds herself orphaned on a planet called Demeter. The recurrence of this pattern should not be surprising; in fact, Annis Pratt amply documents the use of the Demeter myth in chapter 7 of *Archetypal Patterns in Women's Fiction,* and Thelma Shinn details its revision in feminist science fiction in *Worlds within Women.*[14] Despite the varying treatments of the myth, each novelist stresses female alienation and the struggle of women to be reconciled with a maternal figure in a hostile world. At the same time, the appearance of snow reminds the reader of the power of female anger. Like Demeter, women in feminist science fiction develop the power to blast the Earth and to destroy male culture. In postapocalyptic or fallen worlds, women use their reproductive capabilities to create all-female communities. Through parthenogenesis, women can survive without men, but men cannot perpetuate themselves without women.

Vinge's *Snow Queen* combines these patterns more than any other feminist science fiction novel. Vinge interweaves the feminine magic versus male science and also uses the Demeter myth and a more recent version of it, the fairy tale "The Snow Queen." In its thorough revisioning of the myth, Vinge's *Snow Queen* is the most radical attempt to use the material of science fiction to revise its own traditions, including the Demeter myth, which is one element of the feminist utopia that feminist science fiction retains.[15] As she draws together the stories of Demeter and Persephone, Vinge reunites the feminist utopia with science fiction. Feminist utopias, especially the early utopias, valorize motherhood; similarly, in *The Snow Queen,* Arienrhod's cloning of her daughter, Moon, reasserts the tangential role of men in reproduction. In her retelling of the Demeter myth, Vinge reasserts the primacy of woman through reproduction. What was a threat in the female dystopia and mainstream science fiction is transformed into a power controlled by women.

Vinge also uses the myth to show how patriarchy interferes with female relationships. Mother and daughter are separated when Moon is abducted by off-worlders and metaphorically descends into the hell of a black hole where she meets Death: "And Death had moved aside and let her pass" (241). Moon is considered dead by her lover and her mother because the shifting of the planets means she can never return to Tiamat. However, Moon uses her mental powers to traverse this impassable divide. At this point, Vinge revises the myth for a happier ending. Moon is not bound by her experience, as Persephone is, to return to the underworld, but instead she is a Persephone who frees herself, and she even converts the Lord of the Underworld, symbolized by the queen's consort, who dresses in black and slaughters the queen's enemies.

In *The Snow Queen,* Demeter is also represented by Moon's planet, with whom she is reunited, and the lost wisdom of the Old Empire. Vinge uses the Demeter myth in a galaxywide context in which creating life becomes the goal of galactic empires rather than a trap in an individual woman's life. Like Lane and Gilman, Vinge valorizes the powers of reproduction in the public rather than the private sphere. With her crowning as the Summer Queen, Moon banishes the evil female ruler of the female dystopias and replaces the Demeter–Snow Queen with a female ruler who does not need to destroy to assert her power. Moon represents a successful rather than the traditionally thwarted mother goddess.[16]

Other women rulers in feminist science fiction, like Demeter and the Snow Queen, have a mysterious connection with the Earth, including power over the weather. These science fiction goddesses have the same powers that Auerbach describes in *Woman and the Demon:* the "infinite capacities of regenerative being" (17), "the female capacity for metamorphosis" (29), and the ability to draw on Nature depicted as female (38). While in the Victorian texts Auerbach discusses the mythic woman fails to maintain her rule (36), in feminist science fiction the woman ruler's control is unalloyed and even embraced by the readers. The woman ruler has developed the powers of her mind, or psionics, into an alternate science. With these mental skills come a value system that prizes cooperation over individuality, peace over war, psionics over machines, and shapes all depictions of the female ruler. In feminist science fiction, the female ruler often becomes an all-powerful goddess. Inverting this pattern from male science fiction comprises the practice of subverting from within, of using what is inherent in the structure to expose it. Through radical rewritings, feminist science fiction writers make patriarchal stories carry a feminist message.

In a series of novels that she began in the early 1970s, Elgin exploits the possibilities of the female ruler and alternate science. Her novels ostensibly revolve around a male protagonist, Coyote Jones, who resembles James Bond in his predilection for danger and women. However, unlike Bond, Jones is humbled at female hands. In each novel he meets a woman whose psionic powers are superior to his. The series concludes, in *Star Anchored, Star Angered,* with Jones's conversion to the worship of a female prophet whose religion he has been sent to destroy. This pattern typifies the centrality of sexual integration to feminist science fiction.

In *Star Anchored, Star Angered,* Elgin transforms the female ruler into a goddess. Drussa Silver challenges the Foundation with her religious message, which valorizes women and asserts that all humans have the ability to practice psionics. Drussa's bible, which she calls *Woman Transcendent,* exposes the cost of sexism and rewrites women's history. Its first principle is that "women achieve with ease that state of transcendence which men are able to attain only through great effort" (63); its second principle is that "in those times of prehistory when the greater physical strength of the male gave him a certain advantage, he noted the female talent for the transcendent state and recognized it as a great danger to patriarchal society" (63). Drussa preaches this doctrine and gains adherents not in the thousands but in the millions, and she gradually converts whole worlds. The book ends with a female dean of the empire's college assuring Jones that soon the whole universe will be united by this religion. Elgin envisages an entire universe ruled by a feminist goddess and imagines a feminist conversion on a galactic scale.

A Christ-like figure, Drussa transcends even death, and the series concludes with this ultimate valorization of the female ruler and alternate science. Drussa triumphs absolutely and converts the galaxy to her female-centered vision. As in the feminist utopias, the macho explorer converts to the feminine power. Edgar Chapman describes "the martyrdom of imaginative or superior women" as "Elgin's other theme" (94), but it is really Elgin's main theme, coupled with her insistence on the purposiveness of women's martyrdoms. Her female rulers succeed in questioning and shattering patriarchal assumptions through their manipulation of alternate science. This elevation of female ruler to goddess demonstrates science fiction's function as "the mythology of the modern world" and explains its appeal to feminist writers. Through the triumph of a goddess, Elgin's Communipath series makes a feminist transformation of culture seem desirable and inevitable.

Similarly, in *Up the Walls of the World,* Tiptree transforms Asimov's stereotypical frigid, unfeminine female scientist into a goddess of unparalleled powers. Her protagonist, Margaret Omali, is a consummate computer scientist who relishes the cool impersonality of her work and seems to despise humans. Like Asimov's Susan Calvin, Omali prefers computers to human beings. However, Tiptree does not make fun of or belittle this character but gives her a personal history of physical (Omali underwent a clitoridectomy) and psychological trauma that explains her coldness. Tiptree joins masculine and feminist science in this character, for Margaret Omali is not only a superb scientist but an accomplished practitioner of psionics.

Using her psionic powers, Omali contacts and merges with a computer system and a powerful entity, Star Destroyer, an alien capable of destroying worlds. Together they become LIFE PRESERVERS, but while all-powerful now, Omali still appears in human form occasionally and is described as the "goddess of the night" (271). Margaret/LIFE PRESERVER is immortal and has the power to destroy and resuscitate races and worlds. To misogynists, the final words of the novel ominously hint at the female goddess's power and her next target: Her "POWERS MAY ONE DAY FOCUS WITHOUT WARNING UPON THE TINY LIFES OF ANY NESCIENT EARTH" (311).

Tiptree brings the female ruler to omniscient heights and uses Margaret Omali to refute the sexist depiction of female scientists by writers like Asimov and Philip José Farmer. Omali's African-American roots suggest that contemporary feminists in general have abandoned the racism of the feminist utopias. Separatism is belied, as the union of male and female lovers through Star Destroyer shows the disutility of gender, as do the role reversals of the Wind People and the hermaphrodite alien whom the Life Preserver rescues. For the immortal female goddess, tremendous powers and even immortality are to be shared. The transformed woman draws humans, aliens, and even a dog to her. Her new form includes that of humanity, but her larger self is described in terms that evoke a womb. From the perspective of a human male, her shape is at first threatening: "Reach, stretch, get in! . . . he is crawling through a perilously frail dark tube, a frightened astronaut squirming through an umbilicus to the haven of some capsule. Get on, crawl, squeeze, go" (271).

Immortality involves confronting and finally embracing the Other, and Omali acknowledges her computer's life and that of the alien. Being immortal provides her with a new perspective, and those she draws to her become similarly imbued with a vision of eternity and benevolence, "an eternity of unimaginable projects" (298). What will characterize their lives is no grand or specious philosophy but "the old necessity of kindness" (299) and love. The male character, Daniel, who has followed Omali, realizes that "no matter how long the future stretches, or what it holds, he will carry into it his love" (300). This emphasis on community, tenderness, and love is typical of feminist science fiction, as critics have noted (Gilligan 149).[17] What is different about this cyborg and her immortality is that she uses her powers to promote feminist values of community. In this novel, the female scientist changes the universe, and those feminine powers that science dismisses— telepathy, precognition—save the Earth from destruction. Like Elgin, Tiptree creates a modern myth—of a female computer scientist who becomes a goddess, ready to punish patriarchal society. Tiptree simultaneously exposes the pain and suffering that an African-American woman endures in a sexist and racist society and suggests that woman can transcend the limitations of her confining society.

Hugo Award–winner Octavia Butler also uses an African-American goddess to challenge racist as well as sexist worldviews in her novels about the psionic Patternists.[18] That she successfully does so is marked by Haraway's decision to close *Primate Visions* with a discussion of Butler's complexities and importance. Haraway notes: "Like Tiptree—and modern primatologists—Butler explores the interdigitations of human, machine, nonhuman or alien and their mutants in relation to the intimacies of bodily exchange and mental communication" (378). Even more than Tiptree, Butler demonstrates how much feminist science fiction has matured since the racism of Gilman and Lane. She goes far beyond Le Guin's dark-skinned protagonist in *The Left Hand of Darkness,* for her characters derive their psionic skills from their African ancestors, and they struggle to understand and control their powers.

In *Mind of My Mind,* Mary, the product of human breeding by a patriarch, discovers she has the power to control other Psis. But she must overcome the patriarch Doro, a four-thousand-year-old Nubian, and reject the passivity of the matriarch Emma, an Ibo goddess. Through Mary's experiences, Butler covers ancient African history and the chronology of American racism. The psionic skills of her protagonists reveal the folly of racism and sexism, for through their powers the main characters create a new type of discrimination against Mutes, people without psionic potential (the Psis contain a balance of the sexes and races). Doro is shown to be cruel and indifferent to the pain of his family because he lets those who are not strongly psionic live in misery and torment. These latents are unstable, suicidal, and murderous because they cannot control their powers. They hear voices, experience others' pain, become alcoholics, or are institutionalized or imprisoned. Most of the victims are female, reaffirming their greater sensitivity and the cost to women of any deviation from the dominant culture. Mary, who is described as benevolent, cures these defectives and draws them into her hive.

Butler makes the male-female conflict in *Mind of My Mind* explicit through her descriptions of Mary, whose mental Pattern is referred to as "the family" (212). Mary genuinely cares for her "children," and she rules by persuasion and love rather than threat, as Doro did. She creates what had been impossible before, a community of Psis. Previous to her Pattern, the mental presence had been too harmful for Psis to live together. Mary is "a mental queen bee, gathering her workers instead of giving birth to them" (154). Actually, she does give birth, but it is a mental rebirth in which she transforms the ghetto of Forsyth into a powerful and happy community. To the benefit of all the Psis, the nurturing queen bee replaces the patriarch. Even the metaphor Butler uses demonstrates the feminist transformation of science fiction because she reclaims the image of a queen bee as a positive and powerful depiction of a female ruler. As a ruler, and especially as she battles the patriarch Doro, Mary displays the ability to defend her family and to be ruthless in pursuit of autonomy for herself and her family.

Butler's Patternist novels are important because, by incorporating African myths into psionic storylines, they dispel the racist assumptions of the early feminist utopias. Like other feminist rulers, Mary legitimizes her rule through her witchlike powers and her generous use of them. Her conflict with Doro shows that women do rule differently from men and endorses the community-centered values of the feminist utopias. With her power of life and death over the Patternists, Mary realizes the heritage of her ancestor, Emma, who was worshiped as a goddess by her Ibo tribe. In contrast to Emma, however, who passively resists Doro, Mary is an active and successful goddess. Through science fiction devices such as psionic powers, feminist writers create feminist myths to replace the misogyny of patriarchal myths.

Butler's novels represent another important pattern transformed by woman writers. Reproduction, which appears as a threat in the female dystopia and in mainstream science fiction, is here presented positively. Female reproductive power, the power of mothering, is shown to be beneficent when Mary creates a nurturing environment for both Psis and Mutes. In a pattern that appears often in feminist science fiction, Butler shows how preferable mothering is to fathering as a social structure. Instead of the horrific smothering presented in a story like Farmer's "Mother," feminist writers revise the depiction of mothering that fits the new theories of psychologists like Gilligan. Through Mary's success, Butler suggests that mothering can be a way to run societies, not just families. Cherryh suggests the same pattern in *Hestia,* and Lessing uses mothering as a metaphor for the empire of Canopus.

Apocalypse

■ The feminist goddesses who rule as nurturant mothers rather than as authoritarian fathers do so for the benefit of men *and* women; they consider and care for both sexes. In this regard, feminist science fiction differs from feminist utopias, in which female rulers deliberately exclude men from the benefits of their civilizations. Yet, while feminist science fiction is primarily integrationist, it does contain a warning. Repeatedly, feminist science fiction writers draw on settings of apocalypse to suggest the likelihood that patriarchal society will destroy itself.

The postapocalyptic setting is another version of feminist science fiction's mythic revisions. The disaster-ridden landscape can be traced in part to the Demeter myth, for it is usually the Earth that is withered and dying, a collapse often accentuated by snow and ice. These nuclear winter landscapes frequently are caused by masculine science or war. Flawed mother/daughter relationships often are the focus of the plot in postapocalyptic feminist fiction. Simultaneously, feminist writers criticize masculine abuse of technology because war inevitably leads to apocalypse. Female survivors attest to the superior endurance and adaptability of woman. Feminist science fiction's use of apocalyptic settings prepare for Lessing's Canopus in Argos series, in which every volume contains an apocalyptic scenario. Feminist science fiction includes moments or societies that are separatist, but the novels always return to integration and reunification of masculine and feminine societies and male and female characters. By drawing on apocalyptic moments, feminist writers provide an especially trenchant critique of hard science and its global threat to humanity.

One of the most chilling and early examples of this use of apocalypse appears in a short story, "The Heat Death of the Universe," by Pamela Zoline. Interspersed accounts of entropy and the events of a California mother-housewife's day suggest that women cope daily with apocalypse. The intertwined narratives show the reader how the events of a woman's life illustrate the concept of entropy and, at the same time, explain one cause of female insanity in patriarchal society as Sarah Boyle slowly goes mad.

Zoline's fiction brilliantly illustrates science fiction's potential as feminist polemic. No political statements are made, and none are needed as the context of woman and science exposes female subordination. Sarah's story explicitly recalls Demeter's, for as she goes insane, Sarah "thinks of the end of the world by ice" (114). The death of the universe is juxtaposed to, perhaps even caused by, the havoc in her mind. Like Demeter, Sarah destroys the Earth because of her anger at patriarchy. Incredibly, in *Alien Encounters,* Mark Rose ignores the overtly feminist message and uses Zoline's story only to illustrate his contention that science fiction is not formulaic (2). His neglect of the feminist theme of the story is yet another example of the failure of male science fiction critics as well as writers to appreciate the transformation woman writers are effecting. Zoline's story does show the possibilities of science fiction, but, more important, her fiction demonstrates the significance of scientific apocalypse to the feminist writer. The concept of entropy can be used to expose the pain caused by female subordination.

Cherryh uses apocalypse to vindicate another form of feminine power—precognition. In the appropriately titled "Cassandra," the witchlike protagonist, Crazy Alis, spends "a lifetime in and out of hospitals" (157–58). Like Piercy's "woman on the edge of time," Crazy Alis has been drugged and institutionalized because of her ability to see into the future. As the story's title suggests, Alis can only predict evil; as a result, she is even accused of murder when she warns of a young boy's death. At the beginning of the story, Alis foretells the apocalypse, but again people scoff at her, except for one man, whom Alis saves. Her vision of disaster enables her to avoid collapsing buildings and falling bombs. The story concludes with everyone dead except Alis, who finally and devastatingly smiles when her claim "I'm not crazy" (160) has been validated.

In "Cassandra," Cherryh vilifies technology and patriarchal abuse of science. The newspaper headlines tell the reader the cause of the apocalypse—WAR. The man Alis saves ignores a second warning, and so he dies too, as does a male looter who threatens her. Crazy Alis's vision, condemned as fantasy by the doctors, saves her. She remains in secure possession of the postapocalyptic world, and for the first time in her life, she is happy and content. Again, a feminist writer uses apocalypse to valorize feminine power: "Cassandra" suggests that men must listen to "crazy" women or die. Cherryh also depicts woman as a survivor, able through her special powers to survive a catastrophe that kills "normal" people.

Apocalypse is a favorite setting in science fiction, but women use it differently than men. Where male writers use apocalypse to assert the importance of brute strength,[19] female writers show that women are more likely to survive than the men who create apocalypse. Their "insanity" enables female protagonists like Cherryh's Alis to survive. Similarly, Russ's Whileawayans exploit the reproductive powers of the female body and prove what writers of female dystopias fear—that man is superfluous.

In McIntyre's Hugo and Nebula award-winning novel *Dreamsnake,* the planet does not even have a name, so it might be Earth or any other world. However, its anonymity does not blunt McIntyre's message about the dangers of male-dominated science. Like so many other feminist writers, she uses a postapocalyptic setting to valorize female power. As in other works of feminist science fiction, mismanagement of technology results in a blast-ed planet, and the destructive machines are specifically associated with men. The only remnant of the previous civilization is a city, closed off from the rest of the planet. When Snake, the protagonist, pleads for help from the city's vast technological resources, she is sternly rejected by two men from the city's ruling family. The nuclear war that destroyed Snake's planet is implicitly tied to the people in the city, who must be the descendants of those who began that war.

Snake, the heroine of the novel, offers an alternative to the selfish and fearful city dwellers. She is a woman healer who is part of a long tradition of witches and midwives. Although she does not call herself a witch, Snake has many witchlike characteristics. She has three snakes that she uses to cure people because the snakes "are imprinted on her and would stay near and even follow her" (49). Those she helps recognize her "magic" (74, 274), and her skills represent an alternative science. Snake and her people practice genetic manipulation and use snakes instead of drugs, which are scarce on this primitive world. The catalyst drugs in the snakes are superior to pain-killers, "the strong and over-whelming kind that weakened the body instead of strengthening it" (92). Like her fellow healers, Snake is resistant to illness. "I never get sick," she declares. "I never have infections. I can't get cancer. My teeth don't decay" (119). She is the best of her tribe, as indicated by her name.[20] She has also created five dreamsnakes, a great achievement as the species is rare and difficult to breed. A final indication of the healers' magic is the constantly maintained temperate climate of their base, which contrasts strikingly with the desert of the rest of the planet.

As in so many science fiction novels written by women, the woman healer triumphs in this landscape of adversity. The novel follows Snake's journey to replace the dreamsnake killed by an ignorant man, and even without her dreamsnake, Snake soothes and heals many. One of those she heals spiritually is a young girl, Melissa, damaged by a fire and sexually abused by her master. Snake adopts her and provides the opportunity for Melissa to become a healer, for Snake has noticed her "magic" (232) with horses. Their bond emphasizes the specifically feminine nature of alternate science.

The woman healer is a figure of reconciliation, and Snake's gathering of Melissa and Arevin, a young man she meets on one of her medical mercy missions, signals new hope for her planet and the tribe of healers. As in many feminist science fiction novels, the woman provides a unifying force. McIntyre recasts the nuclear family through the bonding of Melissa, Arevin, and Snake. Yet this "family" relies on the independence and strength of all its members and functions nonhierarchically. Their interactions emphasize again the benefits of a feminist approach to relationships for men, women, and children. Snake's triumph over a postapocalyptic world valorizes alternative science and also suggests the remarkable power of women to survive. Her genetic manipulation draws on what is depicted as a liability in male science fiction—the female power of reproduction. In McIntyre's world, reproduction becomes a science that can be used to heal. The setting serves to emphasize Snake's powers and to suggest that, in a disaster-stricken world, it is women who will determine the race's survival. At the same time, McIntyre uses Snake to make a powerful plea for tolerance. Implicitly, she condemns men's treatment of women healers and suggests through Snake how much our culture may have lost by neglecting alternate science.

Indicative of how far this tradition has developed, the power of alternate science is both stressed and decried in *The Shore of Women,* by Pamela Sargent. Sargent reveals that this type of fiction has become well established and confident enough to inspire self-criticism. Like other such works, *The Shore of Women* emphasizes a war between men and women, the power of alternative science, the importance of the mother/daughter tie, and the presence of a feminist goddess. A postapocalyptic setting serves to underscore the dangers of present patriarchal science. In contrast to the unbounded optimism of most feminist science fiction writers, however, Sargent is cautious. In this novel, she criticizes some of the patterns of the tradition. For example, while a feminist goddess controls the male- and female-dominated cultures, the goddess's powers are never authenticated and, in fact, the women shamelessly use the notion of a goddess to exploit and control men. The women also practice an alternative science that replaces the conventional science that has denuded their world.

Yet there is hope, even in the midst of a postapocalyptic scenario. The plot centers on a man and a woman who, despite the obstacles they face because of their cultural differences, fall in love and bear a child—significantly, a daughter. The daughter is given back to the city of women to be reared and to provide an example of another way of life. But the daughter alone cannot provide sustenance for hope—like other feminist novelists, Sargent stresses the importance and redemptive power of art through the written word or chronicle. The daughter is left with her aunt, who then writes a novel to explain to the daughter and to the culture of women what they have lost. The book thus serves a dual function: it warns men about the apocalypse that their science could create, and it also warns women against separatism. The complexity of Sargent's undertaking shows that feminist science fiction has become self-reflexive. In any case, behind this and every novel of feminist science fiction lies the threat of an apocalypse if gender differences cannot be resolved.

This brief survey of apocalyptic settings shows the persistence and purpose behind its repetition in feminist science fiction. Understanding the significance of the apocalyptic setting is crucial to an interpretation of feminist science fiction. By using apocalyptic worlds or even galaxies, feminist science fiction writers attack patriarchy in several areas. First, feminist writers reject the science fiction commonplace that an apocalypse would destroy the gains made by women who should be grateful to male-dominated culture and technology.[21] Instead, woman writers suggest that technology has alienated women from other sources of power, particularly alternate science. Should an apocalypse occur, these writers imply, women would find that they were better suited to survive than men. Russ makes the endurance of woman explicit when only women survive the plague on Whileaway, but her emphasis on the superior survival capacity of women appears in all postapocalyptic feminist science fiction. Feminist science fiction valorizes the strengths of female physiology, strengths minimized by Western culture.[22] As the previous chapter on feminist utopias shows, apocalypse is an important setting for Charnas's *Motherlines,* Russ's *Female Man,* and Piercy's *Woman on the Edge of Time.* These feminist utopias also assert that, in time of catastrophe, women will inherit the Earth. Feminist science fiction incorporates this utopian concept to make the same point that feminist utopias make, but feminist science fiction also offers the hope of redemption from apocalypse and regeneration for men and women alike.

This depiction of women as survivors reminds men and women that women are essential to the continuance of the race, which was an idea emphasized in the female dystopias and traditional science fiction. Theoretically, women can reproduce without men, but men cannot re-create themselves. That which is viewed with disgust and deprecation in male-dominated science fiction becomes an asset in feminist science fiction. Woman writers also extrapolate the physiological fact that women have greater powers of endurance than men, and are hence more likely to survive in a postapocalyptic world.

Feminist writers also use apocalypse as a warning. They point to the dangers of a too great dependence on, and abuse of, technology. Jeanne Gomoll points out that, "integrated into a power structure primarily as victims, women have understandably indulged in dreams about the sabotage of the hierarchy that victimizes them" (14).[23] The hierarchy women writers destroy is not only male-dominated culture but more specifically its science.

Excluded from its sanctum, women are in a position to evaluate its weaknesses and suggest alternatives. Apocalyptic novels do suggest to men that their position is less secure than they believe, and apocalyptic novels all carry overtones of "share the power—or else." As in the Demeter myth, apocalypse is one way women can show despair and anger at their exclusion from science and other powerful institutions.

Finally, woman writers use apocalypse to have, as Charnas put it, a "blank canvas" ("No Such" 26). In an apocalyptic world, women can re-create society in their own image. Apocalypse may be the only way to take women "out of context" of a male-dominated society and value system. Only science fiction offers the woman writer the opportunity to eradicate centuries of sexism and eliminate men from power. Only science fiction allows women to imagine true communities of women or worlds where women have the opportunity to exercise feminine powers and where men might learn to admire and emulate women.

Through a range of strategies, then, feminist science fiction writers reject the simplicity of the feminist utopia. Determinedly drawing upon the blurring of binary categories such as masculine/feminine, science/magic, and science/art, feminist science fiction writers depict worlds in which men can adopt feminine values and in which women can wield science. These revisions occur in a multitude of forms and contexts: through the revision of traditional myths, as Vinge does with *The Snow Queen;* through an increased emphasis on the power of language, as Elgin does in *Communipath Worlds;* through the terrifying ultimatum implicit in apocalyptic settings, as in Cherryh's "Cassandra." Whatever form these feminist fictions take, they stress an alternative to simple role reversals created in feminist utopias. Feminist science fiction looks away from separatism and toward the embrace of feminism and postmodernism exemplified in Lessing's Canopus in Argos series and a host of other feminist postmodernist science fictions that appeared in the 1980s.

Notes

1. *Always Coming Home* is discussed in detail in chapter 6. This novel is not a utopia because it presents a world with both a utopian culture and a dystopian one and focuses equally on the two.

2. Piercy's *Woman on the Edge of Time* contains elements of utopias and feminist science fiction, but because her egalitarian Mattapoisett is set in the future and

is only a possible future, I consider the novel to be more utopian than science fiction. Feminist science fiction, as I use the phrase, refers to specific patterns and depicts worlds in which racial and sexual equality has been achieved.

3. In *Reinventing Womanhood,* Carolyn Heilbrun cites the need for such stories in her discussion of Karen Rowe's criticism of fairy tales (147). In *The Madwoman in the Attic,* Sandra M. Gilbert and Susan Gubar discuss the claustrophobic confines of fairy tale depictions of woman on woman writers (44).

4. The values of the female utopias, as mentioned in chapter 3, bear striking resemblance to the female values of consensus and concern with human relationships over justice and moral rights as identified by Gilligan in *In a Different Voice.* Feminist science fiction amplifies that different voice.

5. In 1983, the Science Fiction Writers of America recognized Norton's achievements when they awarded her The Grandmaster Award for Lifetime Achievement. There seems to be some controversy about whether Norton's name is actually pseudonymous. Roger C. Schlobin claims that "the many citations to 'Andre' as a pseudonym are incorrect" (25). Although he may be technically correct because Norton legally changed her name from Alice Mary to Andre, she describes the situation as follows: "When I entered the field I was writing for boys, and since women were not welcomed, I chose a pen name which could be either masculine or feminine" (qtd. in Sargent, *More Women* xxviii). In addition, Norton has published pseudonymously under the name Andre North. Writers James Tiptree, Jr. (Alice Sheldon), and C. J. Cherryh (Carolyn Cherry) were making similar decisions almost forty years later.

6. Norton's work has been criticized nonetheless for not including sex. In the Science Fiction Shop in New York City, there is a large, beautifully bound book entitled *The Erotic Writings of Andre Norton.* The unwary shopper who takes the book off the shelf finds it completely blank.

7. See Phyllis J. Day's "Earthmother/Witchmother: Feminism and Ecology Renewed" for an analysis of the history of the woman/Nature association in science fiction. See also Susan Griffin's *Woman and Nature* for a lyric exposition.

8. Such conflicts are resolved in Gilman's *Herland,* only to be reopened with the arrival of men, or in Piercy's *Woman on the Edge of Time,* where in the future world of Mattapoisett, women and men co-mother. The discussion here focuses primarily on *Witch World,* the first novel in the series, but the series as a whole is occasionally referred to.

9. Norton's Witch World condemnation of rape appeared over a decade before Susan Brownmiller's discussion in *Against Our Will.*

10. In Sumero-Babylonian mythology, Tiamet is the matriarchal goddess "of the sea and represented the feminine element which gave birth to the world" (*Larousse Encyclopedia of Mythology* [New York: Prometheus Press, 1960]). In *The Women's Encyclopedia of Myths and Secrets* (New York: Harper and Row, 1988), Barbara Walker recounts Tiamat's association with the Demeter myth: "By dividing Tiamat, Mardak [her son] established Diameter (horizon) which was the Greek version of

Tiamat's name, meaning Goddess-Mother" (999). I am indebted to Deborah Byrd for pointing out this parallel to me (see also Byrd, "Gynocentric Mythmaking").

11. In *World's End,* the sequel to *The Snow Queen,* Moon saves BZ, a character from *The Snow Queen,* even though he's on a planet millions of miles away.

12. This pattern also appears, for example, in Marion Zimmer Bradley's Darkover novels, in which a group of women and men work together as a matrix of telepathic power.

13. Lee Cullen Khanna describes "the emergence of credible and complex characters" as one of the most important qualities of utopian novels by women ("Women's Utopias" 51).

14. Pratt does not discuss science fiction in *Archetypal Patterns,* but her discussion throws light on the context of the archetype of Demeter in feminist science fiction. Shinn's useful volume is an insightful look at not only the Demeter myth but also a number of other myths revised by female science fiction writers.

15. Gilligan cites David C. McClelland's description of the myth of Demeter "as exemplifying the feminine attitude toward power" (22) and retells the myth to point to the importance of understanding female psychology.

16. Vinge uses science fiction to rewrite a blatantly antifemale fairy tale, Hans Christian Andersen's "Snow Queen." Like Andersen, Vinge shows a female ruler set in an Arctic land called Winter. However, in Vinge's revision, Gerda (Moon) becomes the new queen and rules beneficently and wisely. Vinge's heroine is allowed both the personal and the public relationship; Moon is both Gerda and the Snow Queen. As in many works of feminist science fiction, settings of ice and snow borrowed from "The Snow Queen" and the Demeter myth reflect the obstacles facing the woman ruler or the woman scientist. Moon battles against the elements as she battles against the male-dominated Hegemony. Ice and snow evoke the archetypal first winter; the Snow Queen's land reminds the reader of Demeter's power to blast and destroy the land and the Snow Queen's power to freeze and mesmerize men. Similarly, Lessing uses ice and snow in *The Making of the Representative for Planet 8* to expose the inadequacies of traditional science. The people of Planet 8 survive through art, which transcends the Ice Age that destroys their planet.

17. In her study of utopias, Carol Farley Kessler discovers that, "typically, women [utopian writers] make issues of family, sexuality, and marriage more central than do men" (7).

18. Butler's Patternist novels include *Wild Seed* and *Mind of My Mind.* In "Octavia Butler's Black Female Future Fiction," Frances Smith Foster describes Butler's fiction as science fiction in which men and women are equal, and she suggests that "for the feminist critic, Octavia Butler may present problems" (48). However, placing Butler in the context of other woman science fiction writers shows that her emphasis is feminist. Like other contemporary feminist writers, Butler's fiction points to the advantages for men and women of equality. In addition, Le Guin prepares us for, and Tiptree follows, Butler's use of major black characters.

19. See, for example, Brian Aldiss's *Hothouse* or any of the other female dysto-

pias, including: Maine, *World without Men;* Berger, *Regiment of Women;* Weston, *His First Million Women;* Anderson, *Virgin Planet;* Wylie, *The Disappearance;* and Beresford, *Goslings.* See also Moskowitz, *When Women Rule.*

20. Snake is a continuation of the Victorian tradition Auerbach delineates in *Woman and Demon* (8–9). Although she is physically humanoid, Snake's powers evoke the lamia/mermaid goddesses glorified in Victorian culture.

21. The vulnerability of woman in a postholocaust world is stressed in such well-known science fiction works as: Ellison, "A Boy and His Dog"; Aldiss, *Hothouse;* and Wylie, *The Disappearance.*

22. As early as 1952, Ashley Montagu pointed out that "the findings of modern science contradict the age-old belief in feminine inferiority" (8); he further asserted that "the evidence indicates that woman is, on the whole, biologically superior to man" (31). Montagu cited female longevity and the ability of women to "endure all sorts of devitalizing conditions better than men: starvation, exposure, fatigue, shock, illness and the like" (58), and included reproduction as a factor in the superior ability of women to survive. In "Social Bodies: The Interaction of Culture and Women's Biology," Marian Lowe cites female accomplishments in athletics: "In athletic events that are primarily tests of endurance, such as supermarathons (fifty- or 100-mile runs) or long-distance swimming, women are beginning to outperform men" (94).

23. David Ketterer makes a similar claim for the function of all apocalyptic literature, which creates "a metaphorical destruction of that 'real' world in the reader's head" (13).

FIVE

The Case of High Art and Science Fiction: Doris Lessing

T he preceding chapters trace the patterns of the female alien and the woman ruler in science fiction that made the genre suitable for feminist appropriation. Images of powerful women dominate pulp science fiction, so no one should be surprised that women writers who grew up reading pulp science fiction magazines should so readily transform the genre. But these writers are not alone; other women writers who belong to the high-art tradition and had no contact with the American pulp tradition also began writing science fiction.

The conversion, often under great resistance, of mainstream women writers to science fiction requires some explanation. Writers like Lessing and Atwood began writing science fiction not in the utopian 1960s and 1970s but in the 1980s. Lessing's conversion deserves special scrutiny because her early switch highlights areas of critical evaluation, involves a series of novels, and encompasses the spectrum of issues that shape feminist science fiction. Her science fiction works through all the issues raised in the preceding chapters, including the move from feminist utopias to more complex feminist science fiction. By deconstructing binarisms and incorporating a feminist utopia into her science fiction series, Lessing resolves the conflict between masculine science and feminine magic. She uses science fiction to comment on human history, particularly the hideous treatment of witches, and she valorizes the power of language and art to challenge patriarchal society. Examining the way science fictional qualities insinuate themselves into her novels and erupt into a science fiction series reveals the attraction and utility of science fiction for women writers. Science fiction subverts mainstream fiction as feminism subverts patriarchy, and this parallel proves useful for feminist writers like Lessing. For her and her critics, the change to science fiction is startling and necessitates a reassessment of ideas about feminist novels and about the legitimacy of science fiction. By employing the conventions of the genre to comment on science and science fiction's gendered blindspots, Lessing uses science fiction to deconstruct the genre itself.[1]

In 1979, Lessing made explicit her conversion to science fiction when she began publishing her space fiction, a loosely linked five-volume series set on worlds affected by two huge space empires, Canopus and Sirius.[2] The time frames and settings of the books vary from a planet very like contemporary Earth to a fabulistic world, and all the volumes focus on gender and psionics. (In this chapter I detail how the Canopus series makes sense only after it is placed in the tradition of women science fiction writers described in chapters 1, 3, and 4.)

Even before she began the series, Lessing was fascinated by science fiction, and her move from realism anticipates that of an increasing number of women who have since turned to writing science fiction. Lessing gradually discovered the narrative opportunities available only in science fiction in the novels that preceded the series: *The Four-Gated City, Briefing for a Descent into Hell,* and *The Memoirs of a Survivor.* In these books, she grapples with the difficulties of accepting a nonrealistic worldview. In Canopus in Argos, she recasts the novel form to create a text that is science fiction in style and theme. She addresses issues that permeate feminist science fiction, such as criticism of traditional hard science; a focus on language as a form of power; the depiction of art as redemption; and the evocation of the characters and themes central to feminist science fiction since Shelley's *Frankenstein.*

Criticism of Lessing's Canopus series suggests that her conversion to science fiction was sudden.[3] Well over a decade before *Shikasta,* the first novel in the series, her fiction contained elements of science fiction—for example, as early as 1969 in *The Four-Gated City.* Most critics ignored the science fiction aspects of this novel, preferring instead to focus on qualities with which they felt more comfortable. The unfamiliarity of most critics with science fiction and the critical neglect of Lessing's previous use of science fiction patterns explain most of the adverse criticism she has received.

Lessing's apparently sudden transformation from a "realistic writer to a cosmic visionary" seemed inexplicable to the *New York Times* writer who worried that she was "tumbling from the pedestal [readers and critics] erected for her" (Hazleton 21). The reviews of her space fiction series range from faint praise to outright condemnation and dismissal and are generally negative; for example, one critic wrote that *The Making of the Representative for Planet 8* "is very short. Thank God in Her mercy for that. . . . [It is] actually painful to read" (Turner 238, 274). Nor can the adverse reaction be attributed in every case to the reviewers' misguided distaste for science fiction. The science fiction critic Patrick Parrinder damns Lessing's space fiction. He writes of her "paranoia" and "gullibility" and insists that she "argues that schizophrenia . . . provide[s] the keys to salvation" ("Descents" 8, 18). Indeed, Parrinder even objects to what he calls the implausibility of the Canopus series, saying that any professional science fiction writer writes more convincingly (23). With reviews like these, Lessing's space fiction appears as homeless as the natives of Planet 8.

Some of this critical confusion stems from pigeonholing Lessing as a realistic novelist. Many readers know her primarily as the author of *The Golden Notebook,* an influential feminist novel—indeed, one of the key feminist novels of its decade—about a female artist struggling against writer's block. Most of Lessing's previous novels were praised for their focus on character rather than setting or symbolism. But her Children of Violence series shows her growth from the writer of bildungsroman to the creator of a symbolic *Four-Gated City,* from a writer who focuses on character to a writer primarily concerned with the social. Those critics who express surprise and dismay at Lessing's sudden conversion to science fiction also have ignored the romance elements of her novels. Most critics agree that the romance form has shaped science fiction, which should be read as a version of romance in which types rather than characters are the central focus (Rose 8). In a series of lectures given in 1984, Lessing herself asserted that "fantasy, the general genre fantasy, has gone on as long as human beings have and was here long before realistic fiction" (Stamberg 3).[4] In fantasy—or romance—the setting itself may become the character, as occurs in Lessing's space fiction, where the empires of Sirius and Canopus function as "realistic" characters.

Like other feminist science fiction writers, Lessing emphasizes writing from the margins. As many critics have noted, the outsider remains a focus of all her work, and female exclusion in particular is emphasized in the novels of the 1960s (Morgan; Rubenstein). Her conversion to science fiction coincides with a renaissance of women science fiction writers who similarly focus on woman as outsider. Lessing was writing *The Four-Gated City* while Le Guin was working on *The Left Hand of Darkness;* Russ's *Female Man* and Lessing's *Memoirs of a Survivor* were published within months of each other.

In Canopus in Argos, Lessing deals with issues raised by all those novels. The series must be read as one text, in part because it represents the range of strategies used by feminist science fiction writers. Like Dorothy Richardson's *Pilgrimage,* it works as feminist bricolage because it uses elements of the science fiction tradition to deconstruct science fiction itself. The form, which is a series of novels, is postmodern and science fictional. On the one hand, it reads as a pastiche, a conglomeration; on the other hand, it employs that hoary standard of popular fiction, the series. Within the series, Lessing draws on forms and themes as traditional to the genre as scientific reports and journals and patterns of the female alien, the Demeter myth, the distinction between hard and soft science. One novel in the series, *Marriages between Zones Three, Four, and Five,* is a feminist utopia, but since it is identified as part of a larger series, Lessing avoids the pitfall of naïve separatism. Simultaneously, the presence of *Marriages* in the series resists the co-option of Canopus in Argos by the dominant tradition of science fiction and the patriarchal culture. True to what the French feminists see as a feminine text, the series contains no ending; it resists closure, just as femininity in a patriarchal culture resists definition.

Lessing foregrounds the issue of language(s) and text(s) throughout the Canopus series and particularly in the last volume to delineate the possibility of resistance to patriarchy. She takes a poststructuralist approach to what she identifies as the coercive qualities of language, and, indeed, the series draws on postmodernism to challenge the linear assumptions of traditional novels. To appreciate her novels, it is not necessary to apologize, as Albinski seems to do when she asserts: "Although fragmentary, they are connected by Lessing's moral vision, which sets them into a consistent perspective" (*Women's Utopias* 131).[5] A poststructuralist approach reveals that a complex critique of patriarchy and writing is sustained in Canopus in Argos. Lessing's series deserves to be read in the context of other works of feminist science fiction, for this framing illuminates the series and more popular feminist science fiction.

Like other feminist science fiction writers, Lessing emphasizes egalitarian principles throughout her series. Like Olaf Stapledon, to whom she has been compared, she emphasizes philosophy as well. However, unlike Stapledon and other male science fiction writers, Lessing depicts men and women as equals. Like Wells, Lessing uses evolution; however, unlike Wells, she envisions men *and* women as evolving.[6] Like other feminist science fiction writers, she transforms the trope of woman as alien; in her novels, the female alien becomes a friend of the human race rather than a foe. Just as Demeter became a beneficent goddess, Canopus, who transcends gender stereotypes and mothering, becomes a power that can be used to rule empires, not just isolated female countries. Canopus presents the possibility of a feminist utopia, while the other empires suggest the patterns of feminist science fiction. Lessing takes from science fiction the tropes of an apocalyptic setting in the near future, psionics, aliens—particularly woman as alien—and space empires. She adapts from feminist science fiction the feminist goddess, masculine science versus feminine magic, alternative science as art, and women and science in a postapocalyptic world.

Interpreted in the context of women's science fiction, Lessing's conversion to the genre not only makes sense but appears to have been inevitable. The patterns of feminist science fiction are perfectly suited to her interest in the position of women, the failures of hard science, and the didacticism possible through art. She devotes a lengthy afterword in *The Making of the Representative for Planet 8* to the polar explorations of Robert Scott, which fascinate her; in doing so, she echoes Shelley's interest in Walton's Arctic journey. Lessing's interest in the recording of an exploration is augmented by her interest in another manifestation of hard science, the new physics, whose emphasis on the volatility and capriciousness of submolecular particles strongly connects it to postmodernism. Its deconstruction of traditional hard science methodology makes new physics feminine *by contrast* because it is decentered, playful, and uncontrolled. Somewhat poignantly, in *The Sirian Experiments* Lessing regrets that "we can't all be physicists" (ix), but her science fiction presents the opportunity for her and her readers to re-imagine the universe, just as physicists do. These two models of science—Scott's doomed expedition exemplified in journals and the playful patterns of modern physics—shape her science fiction and in it become an alternative science that is identified as feminine.

Before Lessing creates an alternative to hard science, however, she exposes the mistreatment of women in the name of hard science. Her critique of hard science first appears in *The Four-Gated City,* the last volume of her earlier series Children of Violence. The series follows the heroine, Martha Quest, from her childhood in Africa to her experiences with psionics in postwar Britain. In the last volume, Martha becomes a housekeeper for Mark and Lynda Coldridge. Through her experiences in the Coldridge household, she learns to love Mark and then to love and understand his "insane" wife. Lessing exposes the shortcomings of traditional hard science in the masculine medical establishment's abuse of the scientific method and technology. Lynda Coldridge is wrongly hospitalized; her visions do predict the future in which an evolution of the human race transcends male-dominated hard science. Although Lynda harms no one, her male doctor tortures her with drugs. Lynda's son writes that "doctors everywhere were on the edge of the truth, . . . but they were badly handicapped by their 'scientific method'" (621), which has become the new orthodoxy. This blindness produces technologies that poison the Earth and lead to apocalypse. In the end, the world is destroyed by the powers of traditional hard science, and Lynda and Martha oversee the education of a new, telepathic human race.

Throughout *The Four-Gated City* as well as Lessing's space fiction, women have special powers and are more receptive to unseen forces that bind the universe together. Intuiting a unified field theory of minds rather than of physical forces, these twentieth-century women have witchlike powers of telepathy and second sight, and they practice soft science. Lynda is described as looking like a sick witch, and she appears with a black cat; similarly cast as witchlike, her friends Dorothy and Mrs. Mellendip have second sight (396, 586, 524). Almost against her will, this fragmented community of women draws Martha in, and she begins to "see" and "hear" as Lynda does, telepathically. The powers are a mixed blessing, for Martha too must struggle with her identity and sanity. Special powers make the women especially vulnerable; like Cassandra's, Martha's and Lynda's gift of prophecy is degraded and made bitter by male authority, and they can only prophesy catastrophe. Lynda is taunted with the title "'nothing-but Cassandra'" (225), the term used by the mental health profession, which catalogs people. Witches are treated no better in twentieth-century England than they were in the seventeenth century, when "wisewomen, healers, and midwives were especially singled out by the witchhunters" (Rich 125); like them, Lynda is ridiculed, imprisoned, and tortured by men of "science" (Rigney 83). However, Lessing's Lynda Coldridge—like Cherryh's Alis, who prophesies disaster, is dismissed as insane, but survives the holocaust she has foreseen—is vindicated by apocalypse. In Lessing's and Cherryh's fantastical narratives, the world as we know it does come to an end, destroyed by male-dominated science, but the women survive.

In *The Four-Gated City,* as in other works of feminist science fiction, hard science inculcates an either/or mentality with concomitant true/false, reality/fantasy, and hard science/magic dichotomies. This rigidity is imposed on Lynda and Martha, who do not deny the power of hard science. They attempt to interest Mark and Jimmy Wood, a scientist friend, in magic, but the men closest to them are slow to appreciate their discoveries. When Mark writes *The City* with Martha's help, he diagrams the cities of Canopus but fails to perceive this empire with female representatives as an alternative. Instead, he rejects his own book as fantasy and tells Martha, "'I want to write about something real'" (185). After the apocalypse, the children practice psionics, which becomes the new standard of communication and definition of humanity, as it is in Butler's novels. In Lessing's evolutionary time scheme, the feminist powers of psionics—telepathy, second sight, and so on—at last come into their own. Phoenixlike, the human race is reborn in the image of woman, from the conflagration started by men of hard science who are like Jimmy Wood.

Through the character of Jimmy, Lessing refers back to Shelley to show the potential of science fiction; but at the same time, Lessing uses Jimmy to expose the blindness of male science fiction writers and their abuse of the genre. Marie Ahearn sees similarities between the Canopus in Argos series and British male science fiction (357–58, 363). However, as her portrait of Wood shows, Lessing has qualms about the mechanistic and masculine bent of science fiction. Jimmy appears more openminded than Mark; the sources of Jimmy's space fiction are not the scientific method, which handicaps doctors, but "old alchemical material, mostly untranslated and lying unused in the shelves of museums and universities" (513). These were the sources of Frankenstein's inspiration, which produced his unique and powerful creation that dwarfed all previous scientific achievement. However, Jimmy's work does not live up to the promise of his sources and, unlike Frankenstein's enterprise, it ends in sterility, in death rather than birth. Jimmy can imagine telepathy only in fiction, and he reacts stolidly to Martha's questions about mental powers. While he works on a machine to tap the powers of the brain, he cannot conceive that Lynda, Martha, and even his own wife have powers that transcend those of his projected machine. Like Victor Frankenstein and Walton, Jimmy ignores the potential of feminist power. His machine never materializes, and through him, Lessing is able to criticize the tradition of hard science fiction and expose the limitations of scientists. In her science fiction epic series, Lessing develops the legacy ignored by Jimmy Wood.

Lessing's first entirely science fictional novel before the Canopus series, *Briefing for a Descent into Hell,* stresses the importance of gender to a possible resolution of the split between hard science and magic (Fishburn, "Lessing's *Briefing*"). The book contains a number of narratives, all focusing on an ostensibly amnesiac and insane college professor named Charles Watkins. The narratives contain different points of view on Watkins's insanity, including his own lucid perceptions of encountering aliens. At the end of the novel, Watkins is "cured," but in the process he loses his originality and vision.

Watkins is a version of Jimmy Wood, but he comes closer to appreciating a feminine alternative to the patriarchal world. What Watkins experiences is a close encounter of the third kind, and the science fiction narrative is clearer and more compelling than the others. By contrast, the doctors' reports on Watkins's progress reveal hard science and Western civilization at its driest and most unsympathetic. As with Victor Frankenstein and Lynda Coldridge, the contact with an alien produces what hard science describes as a mental breakdown. Lessing views madness as "but a stage in the evolution of a conscious, truly sane person" (Rigney 8). Like the protagonist in Piercy's *Woman on the Edge of Time,* Watkins is judged insane by unimaginative and unsympathetic characters and is thus a perfect example of Lessing's interest in alternate perceptions of reality. Significantly, in *Briefing,* the alternate perception has a science fiction setting that provides legitimacy.

Watkins appears at first to be a male version of Lynda Coldridge, drugged and institutionalized, his gender identification reinforced because the only other characters who share his sensitivity to alien forces are two females named Rosemary Baines and Violet. However, as Watkins's past gradually unfolds in a psychiatric file, we learn that he is incompletely feminized and his training may hinder him from completing his ascent with the aliens. Because of his scholarly training, Watkins thinks in galactic terms—he measures time in millennia—but like Jimmy Wood's narrow-mindedness, Watkins's perspicacity goes no farther. Even worse, he chooses to return to a circumscribed existence: he volunteers for shock treatment and "succumbs to the dominant rationalistic belief that technology is the cure for all ills" (Bullock and Stewart 245). This treatment not only returns him to the arrogance the reader has learned to dislike, but represents a setback for all the institutionalized people for whom Watkins has come to signify freedom. Unlike them, he can refuse shock treatment, so his capitulation to the dictates of hard science represents its totalizing, controlling power. Watkins's failure shows that women still make better receptors, and in this fallen world dominated by the scientific method, receptors are doomed, like Violet, to remain Cassandras, ignored and institutionalized. In this novel, Lessing's vision is still limited by the twentieth-century frame in which science fiction devices can be dismissed by the dominant culture as insanity.

Implicitly, *Briefing for a Descent into Hell* prepares for the Canopus series because it criticizes the limitations of a realistic twentieth-century worldview. Lessing's perception is holistic, and to her, the male doctors' emphasis on power and control is hard science's fatal flaw. The doctors' bickering emphasizes the insanity of their treatment of Watkins, whom they diagnose as schizophrenic and amnesiac. As Katherine Fishburn argues, they "are simplistic thinkers who are designated quite precisely with simple signifiers" ("Lessing's Briefing" 52)—they are identified only as X, Y, and Z. The doctors are the ones who are at sea, not Watkins. Their pettiness, as well as the lack of any consensus about how to treat him, emphasizes the growing sanity of his perceptions and of an alternative vision of the universe. Compared to the voices of aliens, the voice of hard science is dull and unimaginative. The aliens lure Watkins like sirens, an image Lessing reinforces by setting his vision in an ocean. The association of the aliens with Ariadne and other mythical female figures stresses the aliens' connection with female archetypes. To the reader, Watkins's "imaginary" science fiction visions are more attractive than the real world of the twentieth century. This contrast explains in part why Lessing began to write science fiction: she found it attractive and more malleable than realism to deliver an optimistic feminist message.

In her next novel, Lessing universalizes Watkins's experience, creating a symbolic narrator, an Everyperson. With *The Memoirs of a Survivor,* Lessing moves closer to the romance of science fiction. No longer is the conflict within one individual, but instead she presents a planetwide catastrophe through the eyes of a female narrator who remains anonymous (to stress her significance as a type rather than a personality). In a world whose social structure crumbles daily, Everyperson takes charge of a young girl named Emily. As their world careens toward apocalypse, she finally learns to trust her visions of an alternate world. The novel concludes with Everyperson, her metaphorical daughter, and her friends escaping into this other dimension. We see the possibilities of a successful witch, complete with a hybrid cat-dog familiar.

In a realistic setting, the narrator, who communicates telepathically with the cat-dog and who sees the past in secret rooms, would be dismissed as insane. Such is the fate of the narrator of "The Yellow Wallpaper," a Charlotte Perkins Gilman story in which a woman sees an alternate female world in the wallpaper of her room. However, Everyperson is a science fiction version of the woman in Lessing's own "To Room 19," a story in which the female protagonist rents a room and decides to kill herself to escape her unhappy life. Significantly, the science fiction context permits a happy ending for the alienated female, an ending that would be impossible in a twentieth-century patriarchal culture. In the disintegrating world of Everyperson, the psionic vision provides the only means of escape from apocalypse. Those hidden rooms, which the narrator sees through a wall, provide a refuge for Emily and her friends, the narrator's "children." This escape occurs only because Everyperson and the children, unlike Watkins, trust visionary powers that provide an alternative to the entropy of technology. In this regard, Lessing's novel can be read as a revision of Shelley's *Last Man*. Although Lessing employs a codedly female narrator, she posits a feminine seer who uses narration and psionics not only to preserve and warn but also to save herself and others from a disintegrating world.

In *The Memoirs of a Survivor,* Lessing reaffirms the centrality of feminist leaders in her science fiction. Lynda Coldridge and Martha Quest are Cassandras, while Everyperson is a Demeter, struggling to redeem her daughter from the underworld—in this case, technological civilization. Emily and her friends break through the devastated winter landscape of Earth into an unspecified alternate world. Like the children at the end of *The Four-Gated City,* they have been given extraordinary powers by the conflagration caused by hard science. Lessing shows a successful Demeter who does not have to compromise with the forces of the underworld and of hard science. Like other feminist science fiction writers, Lessing rewrites a myth to criticize patriarchal society.

In a short story written after *Memoirs,* Lessing moves from criticizing the twentieth century through science fiction devices to writing from the aliens' point of view. The aliens in "Report on a Threatened City" have come to an unspecified city to warn its inhabitants of an impending disaster. In that respect, they echo the survivor of *Memoirs.* Like her, they operate in an alternate world and have special magical powers. They use their minds to travel to Earth, but because they first inhabit hippies, their message is ignored by the authorities. Every other encounter ends in failure and even the Institute for Advanced Studies rejects them. Again, Lessing exposes the blindness of male-dominated science and the superiority of an alternative science, psionics. Unfortunately, its superiority leads to its invisibility, perhaps explaining why *The Memoirs of a Survivor* breaks off when the narrator sees her children enter the alternate world. In "Report," the aliens, like Lynda Coldridge, are ridiculed and imprisoned; and, understandably, the aliens give up and return home. The humans in this story reflect the resisting audience (Stitzell 500) faced by all the novels in the Canopus in Argos series.

The treatment of Lynda, Watkins, and the hippies suggests why Lessing took so long to write and identify her work as, in her words, "space fiction": perhaps she feared the literary counterpart of institutionalization—namely, ridicule and dismissal. As the reviews of her science fiction series show, she was right to fear such a reaction. Perhaps after critics look at the elements of science fiction in Lessing's novels, they will examine her space fiction more seriously. Lucille De View, who complains that "fiction structured as a series of scientific reports is dull" (17), misses one of Lessing's major points, that is, her own criticism of hard science. Nor has any critic mentioned, except with derision, Lessing's version of alternate science, the psionic powers of telepathy, second sight, and levitation that witches possess. Yet these forces valorize the feminine, the outsider; they are respectable topics within science fiction and are a long-standing tradition in women's science fiction. Lessing's adoption of these devices emphasizes that they deserve attention from the mainstream critical community.

What Lessing means by calling the Canopus series "space fiction" and how these novels fit in with the work of other female science fiction writers requires further analysis. The use of the term "space fiction" rather than "science fiction" provides some clues. "Space" is used more frequently to describe the genre in England, but Lessing's consistent use of the word also implies a particular type of science fiction. Space fiction, as Lessing creates it, is soft science fiction, because she is more concerned with the powers of the human mind than the powers of machines. Like Russ, Charnas, and Le Guin, Lessing redefines the male-dominated genre of science fiction. She rejects the mechanistic approach of a Jimmy Wood and valorizes psionics, those powers connected with women in science fiction. The series consistently asserts an androgynous vision. Canopeans transcend sex and, like Le Guin's Gethenians, can be either male or female when they visit the corrupt world of Shikasta. In her space fiction series, Lessing examines sex stereotyping through the science fiction lens of beneficent alien empires. At the same time, she draws on the genre's romance tradition to valorize a feminist alternative evolution. Her novels look nostalgically back to a time when the Earth was ruled by a feminist science that stressed psionics, to a time when language as such did not exist and planets and beings communed mentally. This frame emphasizes the postmodern dissatisfaction with and distrust of language.

While the Canopus in Argos series is fundamentally nonlinear and achronological (the books can be read in any order), there is some justification for considering the books here in the order in which they were published. An overview of the series provides the evidence necessary to appreciate the feminism of Lessing's science fiction and makes it clear that, as the series progressed, Lessing incorporated and responded to her critics' negative reactions. Ironically, examining the series as it unfolds over time reveals how explicitly Lessing rejects traditional linear narration. For example, the tenuous connections between the first two volumes, combined with Lessing's insistence on labeling them as volumes 1 and 2 of a series, requires the reader to work at establishing the connections between novels that are set on completely different worlds with completely different characters. What is important about the series, as a brief discussion of each text will show, is the way in which Lessing uses nontraditional narration and the deconstruction of patriarchal dichotomies to harness science fiction for feminist ends.

The first volume of the series, *Shikasta,* is a compilation of narratives that explain, from the points of view of the inhabitants of the space empire Canopus, how a planet very much like contemporary Earth evolved from an Edenic planet called Rohanda to the corrupt and misguided Shikasta.[7] In short, *Shikasta* is an origin myth, but it is one that defies coherence. Through the multiple perspectives of the narrative, Lessing foregrounds the contradictory nature of identity in the characters and in societies. Through this postmodern sensibility, she creates an origin myth that is feminist in its questioning of the accepted order of Western culture.

As such, *Shikasta* explicitly revises Shelley's science fiction novels *Frankenstein* and *The Last Man* by dealing with the isolation and miseducation of offspring. Lessing expands Frankenstein's story so that the whole human race is Frankenstein's monster. Like the monster, the human race possesses great powers but is unsure how to use them; like the monster, the human race loses its creator, Canopus, and seasons begin on Rohanda when the Lock that joins the planet to Canopus fails and the planet is isolated from it. The plot follows that of *Frankenstein* in its creation of the monster and then its depiction of the creator's corruption and abandonment. The story more immediately repeats Vinge's feminist revision of Frankenstein's story, for in the series, as in *The Snow Queen,* Frankenstein's creature (Rohanda) and its Frankenstein (Canopus) are in the process of reunification.

Throughout the narrative, in which Canopus plays creator to Earth, Lessing exposes the failings of the male scientific establishment. On the abandoned Earth, or Shikasta, one symptom of human degeneration is the worship of the fetish of scientific objectivity (Haraway, "Animal Sociology" 219). Although the breakdown of the Lock cannot be blamed on the human race, humans are criticized for not listening to those messengers, the Canopean agents who carry the seeds of human resurrection in the guise of alternative science. Johor (one of *Shikasta*'s narrators), Lynda Coldridge, and even the native female prophet Sais can see the future, but scientists foolishly scoff at their powers.

In *Shikasta,* Lessing introduces an alternative civilization, one that exposes the limitations of hard science represented by the misguided ideas of

Tuafiq, a prominent scientist who promotes hard science as the sole salvation of the human race. Male-dominated hard science had been "in its beginnings flexible and open" (87) but has become rigid in the twentieth century and makes possible a twentieth-century apocalypse—the setting other feminist science fiction writers also use to open the way for female rule and the adoption of feminist values. In a few succinct pages, Johor summarizes the catastrophe that occurs at the end of *The Memoirs of a Survivor* and *The Four-Gated City.* Hard science provides the mechanism that accidentally touches off the holocaust, supporting the Canopean contention that hard science has burgeoned beyond human control. Through the complex narration of *Shikasta,* Lessing shows that a return to utopia "is possible by the constant expansion of human awareness through the multiple perspectives" (Khanna, "Women's Worlds" 59). The humans who first approach a multiple perspective include Lynda Coldridge and other female agents of Canopus, but as in other works of feminist science fiction, both men and women can adopt feminine values and convert to a new feminist awareness. These special individuals provide hope in an otherwise hopeless, apocalyptic world. Most important, they do so by approaching an understanding of the tenets of postmodernism. They relinquish their obsessions with linearity and control and thus escape the apocalypse around them. Through this narrative, Lessing valorizes postmodernism as a strategy of feminist resistance.

In the second volume of the Canopus series, *The Marriages between Zones Three, Four, and Five,* the apparently primitive cultures are only loosely connected to the Canopean empire. In the fablelike narration about an arranged marriage between people from the zones, Lessing again focuses on issues of gender and psionics. As with all science fiction, the events of the story reflect on contemporary society's marital practices and our treatment of women and witchcraft. This novel also emphasizes art through its complicated historical narration of the marriage of Al•Ith, queen of a feminist utopia called Zone Three, and the patriarch of the male-dominated Zone Four, Ben Ata.

Drawing on science fiction's romance heritage, Lessing reaffirms the special position of women. Female warriors and witches control Zones Five and Three while Zone Three is characterized by the alternative hard science associated with Canopus. The inhabitants of Zone Three communicate telepathically with animals and the women control their reproduction mentally—feminist powers that frighten the men of Zone Four, who consider Zone Three the home of witches (36). Yet the women of Zone Four, whom the men degrade and misinterpret, retain the memory of the same powers in their secret ceremonies and songs. Eventually, the union Lessing advocates between the three zones takes place through the women, but first Zone Three's feminist utopian values are tested and revised by their queen's ordeal. The narrative is told by the Chroniclers of Zone Three, who retell the story to rescue Al•Ith, the queen of Zone Three, from the obscurity that surrounds her legend. The novel changes her from a Cassandra to a prophet who made possible the union of the three zones.

This second book demonstrates the significance of art for woman writers.[8] As writers, women create new myths, retell the stories of forgotten heroines, just as the narrator of *Marriages* does for Al•Ith. The narrator's success explains why Lessing cannot leave the popular genre of science fiction to male writers: in *Marriages,* she argues for a transcendent mingling of the values of opposing civilizations or zones. While the novel emphasizes the centrality of the two female-controlled zones, and Al•Ith's plight is that of all pioneering women, Lessing emphasizes the importance of cooperation between the sexes and the possibility of development and education for both men and women.

At the same time, Lessing revises the Demeter myth in *Marriages,* a revision that emphasizes her use of that myth as the background for the whole series, by combining in Al•Ith the roles of Demeter and Persephone. In an insightful paper, Deborah Byrd argues that as queen of the peaceful and prosperous Zone Three, with her mysterious natural powers, Al•Ith functions as Demeter, even as her actions—the forced marriage, the descent to Zone Four—recapitulate Persephone's role (4). The Demeter myth is broadened to include races of beings: Al•Ith represents all women in Zones Three, Four, and Five. She reunites the zones and educates and softens the harsh militaristic male ruler of Zone Four. Through Al•Ith as Demeter-Persephone, Lessing shows what an undivided woman, a woman in a nonsexist zone or world, can accomplish. This rapprochement between male and female cultures, "a permanent escape from the underworld" (Byrd), is only possible in a universe that does not fragment women by denying them power and purpose.

By using the setting of a feminist utopia, a setting that disrupts the traditional science fiction context in *Marriages,* Lessing incorporates the strategy Derrida identified as "changing ground, in a discontinuous and eruptive manner" (56). *Marriages* does not fit as clearly into the series because Canopus is not mentioned explicitly and its precise relationship to Al•Ith is never delineated. Similarly, the novel ruptures the sense of historical time created in *Shikasta.* By disrupting the tidy, ordered frame of a science fiction series, Lessing alerts her reader to her more ambitious goal of resisting definitions and frames created to confirm patriarchal history and conventional notions of time. She forces the reader to reexamine even the comfortable assumptions about what a novel is. *Marriages* thus sets up a feminist resistance to closure that marks the series as a whole. Resistance to the structure of literary conventions draws attention to other disruptions and assumptions about the patriarchal institution of hard science.

The third volume, *The Sirian Experiments,* explores the Sirian and Canopean empires in greater depth and clarifies the underlying conflict in the series as that of masculine hard science versus feminine art. Sirius represents a more sophisticated version of present-day hard science because Sirians' efforts are expended toward two goals: the conquest of space and the development of "devices that would set us all free from toil" (14). Their masculinity is emphasized by their transportation: the Sirian representative uses a spaceship, while Canopeans travel through space using their minds. In contrast to the male-identified hard technology of Sirius, Canopean science relies on psionics; the Canopeans practice telepathy, communicate with animals, and see the future. Canopus usually has female prophets and even the symbols of Canopean power are feminine—earrings and bracelets rather than laser guns, the conventional weapons in science fiction. In this context, the subordination of psionics and woman symbolizes the degradation of Shikasta. In this fallen world, magic and witchcraft are the degenerate remains of Adalantaland, an island where women ruled in peace and justice. Through her science fiction, Lessing vindicates the myths of a prepatriarchal matriarchal culture.

This novel makes the same point as others in the series, but it does so by revising another plot standard to feminist science fiction: the conversion story of a male-identified explorer. Ambien II, the protagonist, is a high-ranking female member of the Sirian empire, an empire that has uneasy ties to Canopus. Ambien visits Shikasta and with the help of Canopean agents discovers the errors of her empire's male- and technology-dominated culture. Like the writers of feminist utopias, Lessing subverts the traditional misogyny of science fiction through plot reversal. Her Ambien converts from the male-dominated Sirian empire to the feminine values of Canopus.

Ambien's conversion is recorded in the letter and journal form of Shelley's *Frankenstein.* Walton's letter to his sister provides the impetus for and surrounds Frankenstein's story; the framing letters are Shelley's clue to the importance of feminist power in a novel that contains no central women characters. In her novel, the hard science–art struggle resolves in a triumph of art (writing) over science, a paradigm of the feminist revision of the genre. Throughout the Canopus in Argos series, the letters and journals of female characters emphasize important feminist themes about the superiority of feminine perception. Ambien's conversion to the ways of Canopus turns her into a pariah, a Cassandra in an empire identified with Earthly hard science. Like Lynda Coldridge, Ambien is ridiculed, imprisoned, and dismissed as insane. Lessing uses her to show how powerful art and hard science can be when joined, for even the initially male-identified Ambien is overwhelmed by Canopus's rescue of whole worlds and people and its feminist commitment to alternative science and art.

Like her precursors Andersen ("The Snow Queen") and Shelley (*Frankenstein*), Lessing uses the Arctic setting in the fourth volume in the Canopus series to magnify the power of art. *The Making of the Representative for Planet 8* finds the whole planet laid to waste by snow and ice. The story of this ecological apocalypse is told by one of the natives, who expects Canopus to save his race, which Canopus does—but not physically or literally, as the writer expects. Encircling glaciers slowly choke the planet, and no technology can save this race or the world because its apocalypse was triggered by the disaster on Rohanda. However, alternate science provides salvation as the narrator's transformation from scientist-explorer to storyteller preserves the race in the memory of Canopus. While this solution may not be satisfactory from a materialistic point of view, to an artist, preservation in art may be more lasting and satisfactory. In this novel, feminism and art combine to effect a rescue that is technologically impossible. Only a feminist empire could rescue these people in the same way that one artist can capture the life of a planet's people. Like other feminist science fiction writers, Lessing suggests that art can save or preserve a culture, even one oppressed by worldwide forces. For the feminist writer, art becomes a force that rivals technology, and as such it is a powerful feminist tool.

The fifth volume in the series, *The Sentimental Agents,* continues Lessing's emphasis on art and contains a rebuttal to the critics of her science fiction. Significantly, Lessing defends herself and other feminist science fiction writers by drawing attention to the suspect and contradictory use of language. This poststructuralist emphasis echoes the position taken by Joan Slonczewski and Le Guin, writers whose science fiction emphasizes language as a mechanism of control (see chapter 6). The final book in the Canopus series focuses on a conflict between Sirius and Shammat, the evil and corrupt empire that appears briefly in *Shikasta,* over a few small planets. Canopus tries to protect the inhabitants from the false rhetoric and sentiment employed by Sirius and Shammat and, as always, looks to the future to salvage what it can from the conflict. One of the young Canopean agents falls under the sway of false rhetoric, and the Canopeans attempt a cure. In the course of the novel, Lessing criticizes our own culture's corruption of language and its emphasis on sentiment.

In *The Sentimental Agents,* Lessing emphasizes the redemptive possibilities inherent in a feminist vision. As outsiders in their own societies, women immediately perceive the danger of Rhetoric while the men are oblivious to it. The rebels on Voleyenadna treat women as sex objects, but it is a woman who saves the planet by listening to Klorathy, the wise Canopean agent who ties the series together with appearances in the first and last volumes. Only the women have the foresight to accept his offer of a regenerating plant food, and their decision saves the population from starvation. In contrast to the wisdom of these women, the false logic of Shammat is epitomized by the burning and torturing of witches (165). Klorathy reminds readers of Ambien's plight, specifically connecting her to the witches, who were condemned "according to criteria (verbal formulae) arbitrarily established by a male religious ruling class" (165), the degenerate formula of Shammat. This identification of feminist power with witches explicitly criticizes Western patriarchy's extermination of them. Like Norton and Vinge, Lessing vindicates witches through the devices of science fiction, wherein witches and witchcraft are given a chance to rule whole empires and worlds.

In the tradition of science fiction witches, Ambien is a success. She resists the disease of Rhetoric and starts a party of Questioners. Through a critique of language, this last novel reminds the reader of Ambien's function as the questioner of male-dominated culture, the Sirian empire. The importance of her rebellion is stressed by the femininity of Chief Peer, a wise and humorous individual who emphasizes that Rhetoric is a disease to which men seem particularly susceptible because they frequently fall under the lure of words and then use them to justify abuse of native populations, including women. Like Drussa in the universe created by Elgin, Ambien provides a feminist point of view, criticizes patriarchy, and finally destroys it. In her science fiction, Lessing creates the Outsider's Society that Virginia Woolf proposed in *Three Guineas.* While Woolf limited herself to the British upper class, Lessing creates an Outsider's Society for the whole universe, asserting the cosmic and universal importance of including women. Science fiction enables Lessing to reinterpret an important feminist essay in a futuristic setting, giving it wider appeal and influence. Her Outsiders are a huge and powerful society of aliens whose point of view affects the whole universe.

In the last volume of the Canopus series, Lessing's purpose seems twofold: first, she warns of the dangers of beautiful language, explaining why her series does not depend on rhetoric; and second, she rebukes critics of the series, especially those who complain that it is too roughly constructed. Those who decry the disorder of the novels or the series's construction as a whole miss the point of Lessing's critique of patriarchal society. She attacks patriarchal thought and institutions, especially the practice of hard science and the practice of writing. She uses language to draw attention to its corrupting and misleading power and science fiction conventions to comment on the falseness and cruelty of traditional hard science. And she violates conventional literary boundaries of both popular and high literature to focus attention on the artificiality and divisiveness of such definitions. Consequently, her fictions have not been well received or well understood. She has displeased Marxist, science fiction, and even some feminist critics, but her alienation of these groups is one measure of her success at disrupting preconceptions and rigidity. As this reaction suggests, Lessing has succeeded in deconstructing a number of cherished, accepted structures and has pointed toward alternative feminist imaginings. In this regard, she manifests a quintessentially postmodern sensibility that is continually harnessed to the service of feminist challenges to the existing patriarchal order.

The last volume in the series continues the critiques of hard science, science fiction, and patriarchy and reiterates the themes of the first four novels and of all feminist science fiction. Through woman as alien, Lessing provides an alternate point of view with which she criticizes patriarchy. Through woman as ruler, Lessing reveals how an empire based on feminist values would benefit men and women. Through the conflict of masculine hard science and feminine magic, Lessing crystallizes the differences between masculine and feminine worldviews and endorses psionics, a science that avoids the simple dichotomy of masculine/feminine or hard/soft.

Lessing demonstrates that feminist power should not be exerted to lay waste, as Demeter does when she creates the first winter, and suggests that passive aggression is not the proper response to exclusion. Instead, art provides salvation for women. Art rescues Al•Ith, enables Ambien II to tell her story, and saves a whole planet of beings. Rather than attempting to destroy the institution of hard science or reject its stepchild, sexist science fiction, Lessing and other female science fiction writers are reclaiming the genre and revising feminist myths of power. In their universes, reproduction is not a trap in an individual woman's life but the goal of huge empires creating races. In these fictions, women's intuition and their history of alternative healing can become the most powerful force in the universe. Absorption in this alternative hard science represents an ideal, a unified field signified by the invisible Lock placed on Rohanda, a mental force field that joins minds and planets. "We can't all be physicists" (viii), Lessing says in *The Sirian Experiments,* but she has given us a literary equivalent of their work. Indeed, she has gone even farther and used science fiction as future sociology.

The Canopus in Argos series makes readers rethink fundamental cultural assumptions about woman's position, mothering, and hard science. Lessing rejects both the idea that women have no place in science and its opposite, "the logic of domination of technology" advocated by radical feminists like Shulamith Firestone (Haraway, "Animal Sociology" 220). She stresses "revisionist" scientific theories that emphasize alternatives to "dominance hierarchies" (35). Recognizing the important part that evolutionary reconstructions play in society, Lessing uses science fiction to review the human past and future through a feminist lens. Hers is the most comprehensive revision of a feminist tradition that began with Mary Shelley.

Lessing's science fiction prepares us for a new development in feminist science fiction in the 1980s, namely, postmodernist science fiction. As the next chapter shows, the elements that are spread out over Lessing's five-volume Canopus series are condensed in a number of novels that place an even sharper emphasis on a postmodern sensibility and form. As an ambitious feminist science fiction epic, Canopus helps make possible its successors. While I agree with Albinski that "looking back over this period, the outstanding writer of utopian fiction is, of course, Doris Lessing," I disagree with her assessment that "few of the science fiction writers of the 1980s seem ready to follow in the wake of her Canopus series" (*Women's Utopias* 155). As I demonstrate in the next chapter, the Canopus series functions for feminist science fiction as *The Golden Notebook* did for the realistic feminist novel of the 1960s: it sets the tone for a decade and suggests strategies for reclaiming fiction for feminist purposes.

Notes

1. I disagree strongly with Lefanu's assessment of Lessing: "she seems to me to express the worst of both tendencies described above: the stories unfold against a background of imperialistic domination that is nowhere challenged while they treat with some of the more mystical aspects of the 'woman's viewpoint.'. . . Lessing somehow manages to come over as an authoritarian sentimentalist" (92). This chapter refutes Lefanu's hasty dismissal.

2. The five volumes in the Canopus series are: *Skikasta* (1979); *Marriages be-*

tween Zones Three, Four, and Five (1980); *The Sirian Experiments* (1981); *The Making of the Representative for Planet 8* (1982); and *The Sentimental Agents* (1983).

3. Fishburn, in *The Unexpected Universe of Doris Lessing,* takes exception to this perception of Lessing's science fiction. Despite the title of her book, Fishburn acknowledges the importance of Lessing's gradual redirection toward science fiction. For a survey of British responses to Lessing's work, see Bazin, "British Reviews of *Shikasta.*"

4. According to Virginia Tiger, a few months later Lessing repeated this point in a lecture and explained that fantastic literature is becoming stronger because "technology has laid the basis for 'a rebirth of fantastic literature'" (5).

5. Albinski also comments that "such concentration might suggest a continuous narrative, but Canopus is far from that" (*Women's Utopias* 148).

6. Lessing's feminism has always emphasized that men and women must work together. Ruth Saxton reports that in a lecture at Berkeley, Lessing "reminded us that her mother had been a feminist before her and that she is a feminist, but that men and women, blacks and whites, have more in common than what separates them" (7).

7. In "Themes of the Other in Canopus," Shelton explains that Rohanda means "whole" in Hindi, while Skikasta means "broken" in Persian.

8. The redemptive quality of art appears in feminist science fiction, but it is also a pattern that recurs in Lessing's fiction. As Khanna explains, in Lessing's fiction "it is art that facilitates and gives meaning to change" ("Truth and Art" 133).

SIX

Postmodernism and Feminist Science Fiction

Like feminist utopias and pulp science fiction, feminist science fiction from the 1980s depicts worlds in which women write their bodies, and feminine powers and female monsters become revered models for alternative societies and sciences. Woman as alien and woman as ruler, the patterns of feminist science fiction traced in previous chapters, continue to shape current fictions; and comparisons to witches and the evocation of magic define the contemporary female alien, just as she was defined in the nineteenth and early twentieth centuries. But contemporary feminist science fiction allies the appropriation of such patterns to a new concern with language. Like Lessing's fiction, but to a much greater degree, recent feminist science fiction not only provides that nascent female monster from *Frankenstein* with a voice but, through narrative experimentation, also fully realizes the sense of difference she evokes. Recent feminist science fiction writers modernize—or, more accurately, postmodernize—the issues of reproduction, science, and gender that dominate science fiction from its inception in Shelley's *Frankenstein* and *The Last Man* through the feminist utopias of the nineteenth and twentieth centuries, the science fiction art from the pulp magazines, feminist science fiction by writers like Russ and Butler, and high-art converts like Lessing. Because it both continues to appropriate science fiction tropes and places them in a new, postmodern context, contemporary feminist science fiction can be seen as the culmination of a long and complex tradition. The way that it repeats earlier patterns and elaborates poststructuralist theories offers examples of how writers continue to meet the challenges of writing feminism.

Unlike most of the feminist novels of the early 1970s,[1] which accept language as a given, the more recent feminist utopias bear the impress of poststructuralist ideas about science and language.[2] Although Derrida's ideas may seem to have little in common with the popular genre of science fiction, feminist science fiction reveals that the deconstructive model can be appropriated for feminist discourse. Derridean formulations of poststructuralism are the most useful here because feminist science fictions emphasize "the power of speech and naming. They give evidence of the enabling mastery of writing, suggesting a feminist logos that could be set against the masculine logos" (Bartkowski 162).

Many works of feminist science fiction, in addition to Lessing's, support Meaghan Morris's claim in *The Pirate's Fiancée* that feminists have been actively involved in postmodernism. Drawing on new deconstructive theories about language and paradox, feminist science fiction writers use both science fiction concepts and recent cultural theory to challenge patriarchal assumptions. As Lefanu argues, "In literature . . . an act of revolution can be achieved only through subversion of the narrative structure that holds the protagonist in place: a gender reversal is not enough" (35). Through new narrative strategies and the use of postmodernist elements, feminist science fiction from the 1980s lives up to Lefanu's call for radical subversion. Feminist science fiction insists on the dissolution of traditional literary and gender categories, and as it does so, its radicalism brings to a logical extreme the development of the feminist science fiction tradition. Once the female alien and the woman ruler are given empires to run, the next step is to change the way their story is told.

In its challenging of accepted orthodoxy, postmodernism lends itself to a critique of patriarchal society. In general, postmodern art, like poststructuralist theory, stresses paradox, contradiction, and self-awareness. A postmodern culture is "no longer a unitary, fixed category, but a decentered, fragmentary assemblage of conflicting voices and institutions" (Collins 2). Although these strategies of postmodernism are not always identified as feminist, and indeed poststructuralist theories and postmodern aesthetics have been criticized for being apolitical, women science fiction writers do harness postmodernist ideas in the service of feminism. In fact, many critics argue that feminist theory, because of its undermining aims, is a subset of postmodern theory.[3] If, as Jean-François Lyotard suggests, "any received idea, even if it's only a day old, must be suspected" (214), then the "naturalness" of the oppression of women can no longer be beyond challenge.

The radical challenge to the accepted patriarchal worldview presented by feminism can take the shape of postmodernism, and when it assumes this shape, feminists need to appropriate the term for their discourse as a means of legitimation. While postmodernism has been criticized for being confusingly abstract, this is neither an accurate characterization nor a justification for ignoring such a widespread and influential set of ideas. In *Feminine Fictions,* Patricia Waugh discusses the ambivalence that women writers exhibit toward postmodernism, but she also explains the parallels between feminism and postmodernism that feminist science fiction writers exploit: "Both movements celebrate liminality, the disruption of boundaries, the confounding of traditional markers of 'difference,' the undermining of the authorial security of the 'egotistical sublime'" (4). While many postmodernist artists lack specific political engagement, these particular feminist science fiction writers show that the ideas of postmodernism can be used for political ends. Through their postmodernist novels, writers like Le Guin demonstrate the similarity and combined strength of science fiction, feminism, and postmodernism.

Because postmodernist elements lend themselves to the deconstruction of gender, such qualities can be used to reinforce the codedly feminist messages of earlier science fiction. When nothing can be taken for granted, especially language, then every aspect of society and expression must be reevaluated, including gender. The emphasis on representation and on the construction of every aspect of life makes postmodernism an apt place to begin pointing to the artificiality and mutability of gender coding. Postmodernism can thus work in tandem with the new perspectives made possible in science fiction, such as the creation of entirely new societies. As the history of science fiction shows, only this genre enables writers to create worlds without men or sexism. Postmodernism and science fiction independently challenge our society's givens; together they provide a powerful arena in which to criticize patriarchal mores.

Critics like Brian McHale, who discuss science fiction and postmodernism, neglect feminist science fiction's radical and utopian possibilities.[4] Because McHale focuses primarily on texts by male authors, he concludes that postmodernist futures are most likely to be grim dystopias (67). This assessment is inaccurate, because, as this chapter will show, feminist postmodernist science fiction contains worlds that are optimistic, disruptive, and contradictory; they take the visions of the nineteenth- and twentieth-century feminist utopias and make them theoretically complex.[5] By using narrative experimentation, pastiche, self-reflexivity, the breakdown between genres, a fragmented subject, cultures catastrophically disrupted, and a critical approach to language, recent feminist writers test the flexibility of the science fiction tradition. They add to their predecessors' emphasis on gender and defamiliarization a critique of writing itself. By using poststructur-

alist ideas and a postmodern context, feminist writers of the 1980s expand
the subject matter and narrative form of science fiction.

"Poststructuralist" and "postmodernist" are terms sometimes used inter-
changeably; for the purposes of this discussion, I distinguish between the
two. "Poststructuralism" refers to a set of theories, deconstruction being one
of the most widely promulgated, that look at discourse not for deep structures (structuralism) but rather for contradiction, paradox, and multivocality. "Postmodernism" describes a culture that includes artifacts that can be
interpreted through poststructuralist theories, for example, popular culture
artifacts like the television program "Miami Vice," commercials, music vid-
eos, rap music, fashion, and high-culture art like Claus Oldenberg's giant
button, Jenny Holzer's neon signs, and Cindy Sherman's self-portraits of
feminine disguises. Most discussions of postmodernism and poststructuralism, however, have focused on the high art of artists like Barbara Kruger or
Kathy Acker. While these artists deserve the critical attention they receive,
attention to their work has overshadowed similar phenomena in popular
culture. Postmodernism is a part of popular culture too—in fact, the blurring of distinctions between high and popular art is one of the defining qualities of postmodernism. To use poststructuralist theories to discuss only high
art is to distort the parameters of postmodern culture. Applying poststructuralist and postmodern ideas to a mass cultural form reveals that these
texts, especially science fiction, are not only more complex than many critics acknowledge but also that they in fact use the same postmodernist strategies employed in high art.[6] Most important for the purposes of this study,
feminist writers demonstrate that postmodernist strategies can be harnessed
for feminism.

Both poststructuralist ideas about language and postmodern art forms
contain opportunities for feminists to criticize patriarchy. Derrida's formulation, then, is even more applicable to postmodernist science fiction. While
the earlier texts support Derrida's assertion by choosing one tack of resistance or the other, postmodernist feminist science fiction looks forward to a
synthesis of these two modes, a synthesis that even Derrida undercuts by the
dogmatic tone of his description. He argues that resistance must either draw
upon that which it resists or attempt to step outside and then necessarily re-
create the structures of oppression, and he calls for "a new writing" that
"must weave and intertwine the two motifs" (56).

While there are many formulations of multivocality, which is a defining
quality of postmodernism, Derrida's description seems best to fit the binarisms that confront the feminist science fiction writer. Through the use of

postmodern art forms, feminist science fiction elides these binarisms and creates a new postmodern, feminist writing. By adopting neither the extreme of reproducing the structures of patriarchal society, particularly its language, nor the extreme of endeavoring to speak through the body, the unwritable text that Cixous calls for in "The Laugh of the Medusa," these feminist science fiction texts dance through the minefield of resistance, to use Annette Kolodny's phrase. They do so by resisting the hierarchy of the high art–mass culture dualism; and, by resisting facile definition as either/ or, they perplex, challenge, and engage their readers. Recent feminist science fiction thus also points to a way of resolving the choices faced by Shelley when she wrote the accessible *Frankenstein* and the more radical, but hardly read, *Last Man*. Through poststructuralism, contemporary feminist science fiction combines the strategies of these two novels.

Poststructuralist feminist science fiction problematizes language acquisition and the gendered and hierarchical structures embedded in language. Many works of feminist science fiction published in the 1980s reveal a poststructuralist sensibility about the power and contradiction inherent in communication. Most significant, these writers criticize the use of language to create hierarchy and especially the dominance embedded in the practice of science. They challenge the use of language itself and how it is made to reify patriarchal structures. In this way, postmodernist feminist science fiction most completely challenges patriarchy.

The range of postmodernist elements in contemporary feminist science fiction is considerable; some texts reveal traces of postmodernism, while others are permeated with postmodernist style and content. All these texts, however, rely on the patterns of woman as alien and woman as ruler and then add to this tradition one of two types of postmodern elements. The first category of text contains trenchant feminist analysis but relies only tangentially on a postmodern sensibility toward language. Joan Slonczewski's *Door into Ocean* and Sheila Finch's *Triad* represent texts that share an emphasis on language, science, a fragmented subject, and a masculine/feminine societal conflict.[7] A second group of texts further develops postmodernist aesthetics through the form of the books themselves. These texts more fully merit identification as postmodern, for they contain postmodern attitudes and aesthetic style.[8] At the same time, they begin with the female alien and the woman ruler but approach her story from a new angle that stresses how narrative itself confines women. Atwood's *Handmaid's Tale* and, to a greater degree, Le Guin's *Always Coming Home,* are written in a nonlinear, self-reflexive fashion that stresses the breakdown between genres. Le

Guin's novel in particular stretches the shape and definition of what is called fiction, and does so to criticize the narrow-mindedness of patriarchal, parochial, Western culture. Her text is the most thoroughly postmodernist of the four mentioned here because it differs radically from the conventional novelistic structure.

While Le Guin's novel is the most ambitious and consciously postmodern, all four texts demonstrate the ways in which the settings and patterns of science fiction and postmodernist elements can be exploited for a feminist message, whether through an attention to the operations of language as an oppressive system or through a poststructuralist view of language and a postmodern style of presentation. Most important, these works demonstrate the narrowness of cultural elitism to the critic. Written by authors who represent a range of science fiction publishing—from Slonczewski and Finch, who publish with paperback houses that have strong science fiction lists (Avon and Bantam), to Le Guin and Atwood, whose work appears on the more "prestigious" fiction bestseller lists under the imprints of Harper and Row and Houghton Mifflin—these texts represent the ways that feminist writers use postmodernist elements. Finch and Slonczewski both foreground language by linking it to the ocean and to contagion or plague, manifesting a poststructuralist sense of language as a fluid medium in which humans are immersed. While Finch and Slonczewski represent this view thematically, Atwood and Le Guin represent thematically and structurally the same interest in language. If we focus only on Atwood and Le Guin and neglect the more popular texts by writers like Finch and Slonczewski, the extent of this postmodernist and feminist literary movement would be obscured. Le Guin's career exemplifies the blurring of distinctions in feminist science fiction: she began by publishing in pulp magazines, is still reviewed in *Isaac Asimov's Science Fiction Magazine,* but also publishes stories in *The New Yorker.* Her work requires critics to rethink conventional categorizations, especially the false high/low art dichotomy.

While the style of Slonczewski's *Door into Ocean* is not postmodernist, this separatist novel contains a striking poststructuralist bias in its thematic emphasis on the importance of language as a mechanism of control. At the same time, Slonczewski builds on the science fiction tradition through her female aliens. In her alien world, each Sharer is female, autonomous, and chooses a name for herself that reflects the tensions and ambiguities of a personality that shifts over time and place. This use of naming is classically feminist and classically Derridean. Instead of a name chosen by others that reflects a patriarchal ordering, these names change and reflect the oppositions each person finds in her own identity. The names also involve plays on language—puns and other double entendres. For example, Merwen, who journeys to Valedon to understand heterosexual society, names herself Impatient One, and Nisi, who functions as an ambassador from Valan, names herself Deceiver. The Sharers' perception of language shapes their science, and this conjunction stresses a nonhierarchical view of the universe. On the women's planet, actually a moon called Shora, libraries and laboratories are part of the women's homes, which are rafts: "The ultimate library was kept within raftwood; every living cell of every raft held a library within its genes, millions of units within a cell too small to see" (270). Because the women do not compartmentalize, "the whole planet is their laboratory" (215). While Slonczewski valorizes the feminine, she does so through a poststructuralist perception of the determining quality of language to what is considered "reality."

The same patterns of masculine/feminine, science/magic that dominate earlier feminist science fiction shape this novel. The Sharers are an all-female species who share genes with the gendered humans of Valedon, the home planet of the male-dominated empire. But despite their common origin, the Sharers have developed an advanced, forbidden science that is identified with magic. They are healers who, in marked contrast to the greedy Valans, refuse payment for their services (like Vinge's sibyl or Norton's witches or the midwives Ehrenreich and English discuss) and consequently are accused of witchcraft while visiting on Valedon. As one of the Sharers explains, however, "'magic is anything you don't understand'" (138). The Patriarchy, a male-dominated hierarchical empire, is notoriously short on understanding. Because of their ability to perceive nature and name it as part of *sharing,* the female aliens can life-shape or regenerate human bodies, a skill that has only a much more limited, mechanical counterpart on the world of Valedon. Indeed, at first the Valans refuse to believe that the Sharers have such advanced scientific skills, because they have been taught that such science inevitably destroys its practitioners. The Valans, jealous and suspicious, attempt to annex Shora and learn its secrets. Like Victor Frankenstein and the men in female dystopias, the Valans fear and try to destroy the female aliens.

This novel, like the other female utopias, inverts the plot of female dystopias, in which the stereotypical male explorer uses his technological prowess and masculine charm to take over a planet.[9] This pattern is repeated, however, in a poststructuralist frame in which contagion is depicted as a "plague of language." Slonczewski stresses the importance of language, especially naming, to feminist concerns. In this feminist poststructuralist retelling, the Sharers resist masculine science and authority. Furthermore, their resistance to oppression is almost literally contagious and is emblematic of the body itself as a sign, for their bodies—and later the Valans'— change color and significance. In their nonviolence, the Sharers evoke earlier female aliens. At first they practice whitetrance, a version of passive resistance, with the female body turning white and catatonic. When this doesn't succeed, a plague escapes from a Sharer and turns the Valans' skin the amethyst color that characterizes the Sharers' skin. Eventually the Sharers teach the soldiers the importance of "notkilling." At the end of the novel, the general who led the attempt to dominate the Sharers realizes that their way could lead to the end of the empire. "'If every planet in the Patriarchy refuses to be ruled,'" he thinks, "'*we all would be free*'" (396). He is not the only convert to this feminine philosophy. Spinel, a young male Valan, also embraces the Sharers' values, and he decides to stay on the moon with the Sharer with whom he has fallen in love. The soldiers who were meant to enforce Patriarchal rule similarly refuse to kill.

In *A Door into Ocean,* the Demeter-Persephone myth, in which a mother expresses her anger at being isolated from her daughter who has been abducted by a man, works both similarly and differently than it does in earlier feminist science fiction. The Sharers co-mother in a manner not unlike the co-mothering in Piercy's *Woman on the Edge of Time*. They merge ova, as do Russ's female aliens in *The Female Man,* and stress the importance of mothers and daughters working together. This is most evident when the daughters are held hostage by the Patriarchal troops and, though they are children, stage a hunger strike until they are released. The myth is not reenacted overtly, as it is in so many other female utopias, but Slonczewski does stress the connection of mother to daughter through the maternal relationship of species rather than individuals. The emphasis on oceanic merging and its linkage to language appears on an interplanetary scale, emphasizing its importance. The Demeter-Persephone myth appears, then, in the stories of the two planets and the two species. The Sharers and Valans are genetically identical, but they have separated from each other because of the Brother wars that divided the Empire and created the remnant empire, the Patriarchy. The novel details the reunion of the two worlds, the reunification of the species through Spinel (a Valan) and Lystra (his Sharer lover), evoking a similar reunion in Gilman's *Herland*. In this sense, Slonczewski holds out the possibility of communication between the feminine and the masculine, provided the latter relinquishes control over language and science.

Finch too creates a conflict between cultures identified as masculine and feminine and draws on other patterns from earlier feminist science fiction, especially the Demeter myth and alternate science. In *Triad,* she points to the way that gender differences are maintained through language. Like Elgin, Finch draws on linguistics to discuss gender, language, and perception and their effect on culture. The epigraphs to *Triad,* from Lewis Thomas and William Burroughs, direct the reader to the central theme of the text, namely, defamiliarization and gender. At the same time, the incorporation of two such diverse writers—a liberal humanist and a radical experimentalist known for his depictions of violence toward women—creates the feel of pastiche. What holds the book together is the emphasis on the construction of language. The epigraph attributed to Thomas states: "Language is, like nest-building or hive-making, the universal and biologically specific activity of human beings. We engage in it continually, compulsively, and automatically. We cannot be human without it." Here, Finch alludes to gender; throughout the plot the nest-building and the hive-making of the female characters and the female computer are coterminous with the deconstruction of patriarchal language and the construction of an alien language that does not stress hierarchy or any of the conventional, scientific ways of describing reality available to humans. Finch stresses how language determines reality and how language is gender-coded through a group of aliens who are quintessentially other.

With the Burroughs epigraph—"'Language is a virus from outer space'"— Finch draws attention to the ways in which aliens and alienation are used to defamiliarize language. The Ents have a language that in fact turns out to be contagious, and once Gia Kennedy, the xeonlinguist who is hardwired to a computer, contacts the Ents, she can no longer regard her male-dominated, mechanically dependent culture in the same uncritical way. She becomes aware that there are pluralities of knowledge and knowledge acquisition. After she experiences the world through Ent eyes, Gia realizes, *"language is the filter through which we perceive reality"* (111). This realization enables her to see the mechanism of control that operates when the humans rename the planet in their language. It also forces her to reexamine her cultural attitudes toward gender, which are overtly determined by the words available to define male and female roles. The Ents present a version of what Cixous calls *l'écriture féminine.* Cixous describes "feminine writing" as "these waves, these floods," in contrast to the male "history of writing [which] is confounded with the history of reason" ("Medusa" 246, 249). "Sweeping away syntax . . . we are at the beginning . . . of a process of becoming in which several histories intersect with one another" (256, 252). This "language of 1,000 tongues which knows neither enclosure nor death" (260) is evoked by the Ent language, which is "an ocean of pure thought—not broken up into little parcels of meaning, logical, sequential, as all the levels of Inglis [English] necessarily were! All of this language was present in any one part. . . . There was no past or future" (Finch 10, 78).

This language is part of a postmodernist practice that defies conventional definitions of science. Like the Sharers' language in *A Door into Ocean,* the differences in the Ents' language enable their alternative science. Like Shelley's Frankenstein, Gia discovers that the alternative science dismissed as magic is indeed powerful and effective. "Mystics and shamans" (23) had produced altered states, but psychochemists and then, to an even greater degree, the Ents use apparently magical drugs to induce expanded perceptions, or hypersensitivity. Significantly, these effects are achieved by the aliens through a feminized symbol, jewelry. Like Norton and Lessing, Finch accords jewelry a special status equivalent to advanced weaponry in traditional science and science fiction. The crew is skeptical about the value of these apparently worthless trinkets, but the Cencom, the central computer, recognizes their value and their hallucinatory side effects. In this regard, Finch demonstrates that cyberpunk science fiction need not be exclusively male or misogynistic. She takes the science fiction trope of the fusion of machine and human, with the particular cyberpunk emphasis on computer software and the human body, and uses it in a feminist framework. Eventually Gia adopts an altered view of the universe and converts in a mystical ceremony to the ways of the Ents—a conversion that is actually part of a test of the human race by an advanced species. In the end, Gia and her male lover return to Earth with the news of a new order of reality.

Gia's conversion is very similar to that which occurs in Slonczewski's *Door into Ocean,* and it appears in the context of a number of tessellated and fragile mother-daughter relationships, which again evoke the myth of Demeter and Persephone. Like Slonczewski, Finch repeats salient features of the myth's revision in earlier feminist science fiction. First there is the symbolic mother-daughter relationship of the advanced species that is testing the humans. There is a union at the end of the book that amounts to a reconciliation, analogous to the rapprochement between representatives of Valedon and Shora at the end of *A Door into Ocean* and reminiscent of similar reunions in *The Snow Queen, The Female Man,* and other earlier feminist texts. The humans now become part of an advanced group of creatures from whom they had been separated because of their dependence on machines. Here again Finch appropriates cyberpunk notions for feminist ends, and the resultant mix alters both feminist science fiction and cyberpunk. On a less galactic level, the computers themselves function as mothers to the humans (14), but they are mothers who care enough for their daughters to realize that they must become semiautonomous. Gia separates from the only mother she has ever known, Cencom, but returns at the end of the novel, self-aware and revitalized. Through the return of her menstrual cycle and her self-impregnation, Gia recovers for Cencom the biological part of its cyborg and reintegrates its divided loyalty. As in Slonczewski's novel, however, reintegration is presented as possible only after the characters confront the power of language and reject the hierarchy instituted by patriarchal language and patriarchal science.

These two novels contain the familiar figure of the female alien, but in both she is allied with poststructuralist ideas about language, especially its ability to skewer and overdetermine perceptions. Through the combination of an alternative science, familiar from earlier feminist science fiction, and a critique of language, Finch and Slonczewski attack patriarchal society. The next group of novels discussed here not only contain alternative science, female aliens, and elements of postmodern style but also subtly direct our attention to language as structuring the form of the book. As characters discover how language structures perceptions of reality, readers must consider their own restrictions and formations in and through language. Slonczewski's and Finch's texts look back to the tradition of feminist science fiction, but they also point forward to an even more overt use of structure by Atwood and Le Guin.

The power of language to oppress and the necessity of exposing its contradictory nature appear in Atwood's concerns about her science fiction novel *The Handmaid's Tale:* "I delayed writing it for about three years after I got the idea because I felt that it was too crazy" (qtd. in Rothstein). Atwood draws on the centrality of reproduction and the setting of a postapocalyptic world to create her dystopia. *The Handmaid's Tale,* like Charnas's *Motherlines* and Russ's *Female Man,* imagines a world in which men and women lead segregated lives and create their own cultures. The novel reverses the female dystopian pattern of Bulwer-Lytton's *Coming Race,* in which a male explorer discovers and then escapes from a female-dominated world; instead, Atwood's anonymous female protagonist is trapped in a world dominated by men, a world in which women are restricted more severely than in our own society. Like the male protagonists from the female dystopias, however, Atwood's heroine escapes, at least from the Commander's house;

and as in the female dystopias, the narrative functions as a warning. Atwood herself asserts the optimism of the conclusion: "The possibility of escape exists. A society exists in the future which is not the society of Gilead and is capable of reflecting about the society of Gilead in the same way that we reflect about the 17th century. Her [the protagonist's] little message in a bottle has gotten through to someone—which is about all we can hope, isn't it?" (qtd. in Rothstein). These comments point to a poststructuralist skepticism about absolutes of any kind. Feminists can take comfort, however, in the fact that postmodern feminist science fiction can get through and that there are enough texts to constitute more than "a little message."

The future society that Atwood refers to appears in an appendix entitled "Historical Notes." Readers learn that the narrative we have just finished reading exists only as a transcription of cassette tapes. Our sense of accuracy and univocality is thus ruptured, and the uncertainty of the ending—does the heroine escape?—is accentuated. The unreliablilty of language is stressed, and our responsibility to complete the text is foregrounded. This principle of uncertainty is stated by the narrator, who exposes the conventions of writing: "If it's a story I'm telling," the Handmaid explains, "then I have control over the ending. Then there will be an ending, to the story, and real life will come after it. I can pick up where I left off. It isn't a story I'm telling" (39). Bartowski agrees, stressing that "as a fiction of a fragmented self *The Handmaid's Tale* offers many strategies that put its status as a narrative into jeopardy" (135). As it does so, the novel points to the ways that language is and can be used to oppress women. Control of language means control of one's life, but in the postapocalyptic world she inhabits, the Handmaid cannot write her story because writing is forbidden to women. Through the censorship of the future, Atwood connects writing to the oppression of women. If this were her only point, her novel need not be considered science fiction. But because her poststructuralist approach builds on the science fiction tropes of the female dystopia, a fragmented self, and a postapocalyptic world, her novel belongs to this feminist tradition.

Once the feminist writer confronts the structures inherent in language, the next step is to imagine alternatives to those coercive structures. A number of feminist science fiction writers opt for a postmodern form as the only way to challenge dominant cultural forms such as patriarchy. In *Always Coming Home,* Le Guin draws on feminist science fiction, but she also stretches the form of the novel as she employs poststructuralist ideas about language. It is a difficult book to write about, for in its multivocality and multiplicity it resists facile definition. The text provides a perfect example of what Jim Collins describes as quintessentially postmodern: "the emphasis placed on juxtapositions of conflicting discourses" (137). Naomi Jacobs explains that the text "combines all literary genres and some scientific ones, as well as music and drawing" (37). This description only hints at the complexity and sophistication of the text, for Le Guin does not provide a linear narrative but rather a compilation of material, including a cassette tape of music and poetry, purportedly a product of the people about whom she writes. Through the amalgamation of diverse materials, she emphasizes the act of interpretation. Even the title page announces the text as a collaborative effort, for it identifies Le Guin as the author but also credits a composer, Todd Barton, an artist, Margaret Chodos, and a geomancer, George Hersh. In depicting the life of a people who "might be going to have lived a long, long time from now in Northern California" (xiii), Le Guin casts her stories as future anthropology, which emphasizes that all acts of reading or interpretation are themselves constructions and fictions. Khanna rightly reads the novel's structure as a return to Le Guin's roots in anthropology, but it is an anthropology altered by her deft handling of postmodernist ideas ("Women's Utopias" 151). Khanna also sees this book as a culmination of feminist science fiction, and she praises the verisimilitude created by the assemblage of materials.

Le Guin's text epitomizes a strategy that McHale describes as typical of postmodernist fiction: "the strategy of injecting a specialized register of language into a homogeneous discourse-world, as a means of inducing polyphony" (168). He stresses the radical nature of this type of narrative strategy, including a more specialized version that he calls "antilanguage." In *Always Coming Home,* the poetry and music of the Kesh function as antilanguage. It is, as McHale says, "inherently *dialogic,* in Baxtin's [*sic*] sense of the term, conducting an implicit polemic against the standard language and its world-view" (168). In an interview with Larry McCaffery, Le Guin makes explicit how the collaborative process of creating the book echoes its content. She describes the process of collaboration as "a very 'Kesh' process of working collaboratively, nonhierarchically—everybody 'dancing together'" (173). Elsewhere, she acknowledges the radical nature of her narrative weave when she explains, "If the Kesh verse does nothing else, at least it spits in the eye of Papa Lacan" (*Dancing* 187).

Postmodernist devices allow Le Guin to attack poststructuralism where it is used to oppress women. At the same time that it is postmodernist, the language is self-consciously feminist. *Always Coming Home* is written in what Le Guin describes as "the mother tongue": "It is primitive: inaccurate, unclear, coarse, limited, trivial, banal. It's repetitive, the same over and over, like the work called women's work; earthbound, housebound. . . . The mother tongue, spoken or written, expects an answer. It is conversation . . . The mother tongue is language not as mere communication but as relation, relationship. It connects. It goes two ways, an exchange, a network" (*Dancing* 149). Postmodernism legitimates and provides space for a text to be written in the mother tongue; and, as it does so, it creates a space for the female alien and the woman ruler in which even the style of the text reinforces and promotes a feminist message.

In *Always Coming Home,* Le Guin employs nonlinear narrative, pastiche, self-reflexivity, and a breakdown of distinctions between genres. Most important, she draws on the qualities of postmodernism to critique patriarchal culture, especially science, and to present an alternative that from a patriarchal perspective must be identified as feminine. *Always Coming Home* is the kind of feminist text that Cixous and Clément call for in *The Newly Born Woman:* "Somewhere every culture has an imaginary zone for what it excludes, and it is that zone that we must try to remember *today*" (6). They suggest the need for a writing of the female body that is "not erection . . . but diffusion" (88). Le Guin's novel does both, and it can be read as exemplifying the qualities of postmodernism through the aegis of "the way texts write themselves/are written now." As Luce Irigaray describes it, "her sexuality, always at least double, goes even further: it is plural" (*This Sex* 48).

Le Guin defines feminist resistance similarly—so much so, that Irigaray seems to be writing about *Always Coming Home.* "The issue is not one of elaborating a new theory of which women would be the *subject* or the *object*," she declares, "but of jamming the theoretical machinery itself, of suspending its pretension to the production of a truth and of a meaning that are excessively univocal" (*This Sex* 78). Through the multivocal and multimedia exposition of her text, Le Guin simultaneously shatters the illusion of univocality and the illusions of patriarchal discourse. Tom LeClair writes: "Le Guin departs from a linear ordering to simulate simultaneity, process, and reciprocity, which make an orderly critical response difficult" (210). One of the many ways that she exposes the imposition of linearity and its cost, particularly to women, is through the autobiographical narrative of Stone Telling, who, like Atwood's Handmaid, finds herself in an alien, male-dominated culture. Unfortunately, to single out this narrative is to do the text a disservice, and it must be stressed that this interpretation is but one thread of a complex weave. (Acknowledging the incomplete nature of this discussion, it must be noted, is being faithful to the feminist postmodernism Le Guin espouses.)

Stone Telling's autobiography is compelling as a story, but, though the reader begins to care very much for her as a character, she carries symbolic significance that transcends traditional storytelling considerations and underscores her role as a representative of a gendered conflict and as the female alien who chooses alternative science. As the daughter of a Village woman and the Commander of the Condor army, Stone Telling (who begins her life as North Owl, but later, as with the Sharers in *A Door into Ocean,* names herself to reflect her life) is situated between two value systems identified from the very beginning as feminine and masculine. The Village exemplifies the values articulated by feminist critics such as Gilligan,[10] Irigaray, and Cixous and represented in female utopias and feminist science fiction: the Villagers value cooperation, communication, harmony with nature. In contrast, the Condor value hierarchy and dominance of the natural world. Significantly, neither society is antitechnological, but each perceives technology differently. In a trope from feminist science fiction, the world is postapocalyptic, a world marked by "the permanent desolation of vast regions through the release of radioactive or poisonous substances, the permanent genetic impairment" (159). In this setting so familiar in feminist science fiction, the feminine society adapts better than the hidebound masculine culture. The origin myth in which this description appears explains that these ancestors had their heads on backwards; to the reader of Stone Telling's autobiography, it is clear that the Condor also have their heads on backwards. As Stone Telling explains, the Condor have advanced weapons of war, but "they are killing themselves and starving" (358). They confront the Villagers when they arrive to build a bridge, but they are building the bridge to reach new lands to conquer and they do not ask the Villagers if there is a need for a bridge before they start flexing their technological muscles.

The contrast between the feminine and masculine attitudes toward science is characterized in terms used throughout science fiction as gender-inflected: soft and hard. Le Guin plays with previous science fiction writers' (and critics') use of the term as she applies it to the two cultures she creates. This view of the Condor's obdurance is corroborated by one of their women who moves to the Village and explains that, with the Condor, "everything was hard; being was hard. Here it's soft" (366). Her terminology evokes the distinctions made between hard and soft science, distinctions that are repeated in one of the appendixes, which explains the medical practices of the Villagers. These practices are reminiscent of witchcraft, a distinction borne out by Stone Telling's experience with a Condor doctor. She is drugged by him and he treats her "half jokingly contemptuous" because she is female;

when he discovers that she was "menstruating he became nervous and disgusted, as if [she] bore some dreadful infection" (344). In the Village, she explains, she would not have become ill at all, but if she were ill, she would have been treated with songs and with a "bringing in," a mental healing. Her experiences echo those of earlier female aliens such as Norton's and Vinge's witches or Piercy's and Lessing's heroines. But where the earlier characters' sufferings are unameliorated, here the narrative style itself corroborates Stone Telling's feminist point of view.

The masculine and feminine societies' differing attitudes toward science are reflected in their attitudes toward language, and again the distinctions are gender based. To the Condor, "writing is sacred" (189), but in a negative, dominating sense. Only Condor warriors are allowed to write; and, as in the Handmaid's world, writing is forbidden to women and lower-class men. Thus hierarchical distinctions and power structures are maintained, but, as Stone Telling describes it, at the cost to the Condor of their souls. Hierarchy and dominant structures exclude women. "Girls and women were taught nothing but the skills of the household. . . . women have no part in the intellectual life of the Dayaos [the Condor]; they are kept in, but left out" (200). Stone Telling experiences these restrictions firsthand when she chooses to live with her father, but because she was brought up by her mother, she is able to criticize and reject the Condor's way of life. Though she despises most of the women for participating in these structures, she attests to their degrading effect. Living with "a people who believed that animals and women were contemptible and unimportant, I had begun to feel that what I did was indeed unimportant" (345–46). Fortunately, the reader of her autobiography and of the text does not concur because Le Guin's insists on the significance of the feminine.

The fragmentation of the autobiography into different sections divided by other tales and information about the peoples provides the reader with additional structures of resistance to the Condor's misogyny as well as the misogyny of our own culture. We are compelled to experience resistance to patriarchal linearity in so small and yet so compelling an act as turning pages out of sequence to complete Stone Telling's story: to follow her autobiography, we must skip ahead and consciously decide to privilege her story over the others. In doing so, we are implicated in the type of coercion that the Condor apply to the people they dominate. Discovering this linearity involves our culture in the critique. We cannot read the text and remain distanced or comfort ourselves with the thought that the Condor are oppressive but that our culture is superior.

The multivocality and nonlinearity of the text constantly remind us of how forced and contrived our customary reading experiences are. As Khanna emphasizes, Le Guin's text calls for active reading: "Whether we are invited, cajoled, teased, 'gently' addressed, assaulted, or left hanging and forced to pick up the pieces, we are involved" ("Women's Utopias" 136). Stone Telling's story breaks off at seemingly arbitrary points, but in each instance we are informed of the page on which the story resumes and invited to decide whether to continue linearly or to resist the flow of the autobiography. Either way, we are made aware that every reading involves choices. Le Guin further stresses the linearity of conventional novels by breaking up the page format with drawings and maps. Nonlinearity also becomes an issue for her future archaeologist, who collects the material but faces a dilemma about how to present it: "a story has a beginning, a middle, and an end, Aristotle said, and nobody has proved him wrong yet and that which has no beginning and no end but is all middle is neither story nor history. What is it, then?" (163). One answer to this question is that the text so described is feminist postmodernist science fiction.

Le Guin expands postmodernist feminism, though, to be the principle of a whole culture. This aspect is stressed through one of the Villagers, who has imbibed the principle of uncertainty that is identified as feminine by French feminists like Cixous and Irigaray. The Villager "doesn't perceive time as a direction, let alone a progress, but as a landscape in which one may go any number of directions, or nowhere. He spatialises time; it is not an arrow, nor a river, but a house, the house he lives in. One may go from room to room and come back. To go outside, all you have to do is open the door" (171–72). This aptly describes the experience of reading the novel. While Native American culture provides one source for this alternative view of time, Le Guin frames the description with the Villagers' feminine culture presented in contrast to the orderly masculine world of the Condor. Furthermore, Le Guin's choice of words makes it clear that it is the masculine arrow being left behind and the masculine perception of linearity and univocality that is being rejected.

Le Guin's description of the Villagers' reaction to time could serve as well as a description of postmodernism, suggesting that postmodernist ideas can be imbued with political intent. She trenchantly uses postmodernism to criticize aspects of patriarchal culture, employing gender distinctions identified by Kristeva: "'Father's time, mother's species,' as Joyce put it; and indeed, when evoking the name and destiny of women, one thinks more of *space* generating and forming the human species than of *time,* becoming or

history" (Kristeva 33). Like Kristeva, Le Guin argues that notions of time
and history are linear and male-dominated—a postmodernist perception
borne out in the form and the function of *Always Coming Home*.

The self-reflexivity inherent in the passage about the Villagers' view of
time is one of the hallmarks of postmodernism. Throughout the text, Le
Guin focuses on the acts of reading and writing and problematizes them.
Her narrator, Pandora, worries about how to represent another culture, how
to convey information. As Jacobs explains, Pandora may or may not be the
editor of the book—even the idea of a narrator is undercut (42). Le Guin's
pattern recalls the uncertainty about the narrator of *The Handmaid's Tale*,
whose voice survives only in the transcription of cassette tapes. Jacobs
praises the destabilization that Le Guin creates but does not identify it as
postmodern. The compilation is a pastiche that stresses the breakdown between genres, which is a defining quality of postmodernism. The text cannot be fixed because it contains autobiography, fable, history, poetry, an
excerpt from a novel, plays (identified as improvisational), a glossary, a dictionary, how-to manuals, recipes, descriptions, charts, drawings, maps,
musical notation, and a cassette of the music and poetry of the Kesh. In this
unique manner, Le Guin realizes the "new writing" that Derrida calls for.
Her text does indeed "weave and intertwine the two motifs," and in it, "several languages must be spoken and several texts produced at the same time"
(Derrida 56). From these diverse materials we are invited to create our own
text and our own home. Le Guin here avoids the distinction made by Derrida between the two forms of resistance—leaving the master's house and
remaining inside, for both are possible within her framework and both can
be a feminist's place. With this flexibility, she encompasses the female utopia and feminist science fiction.

Le Guin's postmodern text demonstrates the unique possibilities for feminists of allying the openness of science fiction with postmodernism. Her
text forces the reader to reexamine conventional ideas about the boundaries
of texts and, concomitantly, the gendered assumptions about language and
science. With postmodernism and feminism in mind, we can look again at
Lessing's Canopus in Argos series of five novels as one text. With Le Guin's
broadening of the frame of feminist science fiction, new ways of reading
and thinking are required. In a postmodern culture, using postmodernist elements may be the best and perhaps only way to resist patriarchal hegemony. As Lefanu argues, "an act of revolution can be achieved only through a
subversion of the narrative structure that holds the protagonist in place: a
gender reversal is not enough" (35). Or, as Le Guin explains, "I don't think

we're ever going to get to utopia again by going forward, but only round-about or sideways; because we're in a rational dilemma, an either/or situation as perceived by the binary computer mentality, and neither the either nor the or is a place where people can live" (*Dancing* 98).

With the framework of poststructuralism and postmodernism, the accomplishments of 1980s science fiction by women can be seen far more clearly. It builds on the tradition of gender that has always been part of science fiction. Like their predecessors, these writers appropriate the tropes of science fiction, including an all-female world, the female alien, alternative science, the Demeter myth, and postapocalyptic settings, to discuss gender. Contemporary texts use the woman as alien and as ruler, but they expand her powers and awareness into the area of language. *A Door into Ocean, Triad, The Handmaid's Tale,* and *Always Coming Home* demonstrate the complexity and sophistication of this fiction. Feminist postmodernist science fiction realizes the tenets of postmodernism as it exposes the arbitrariness of distinctions between high and low art. In its breakdown of categories and its challenge to conventional pieties of literary criticism and even feminism (popular art inherently oppresses women), feminist postmodernist science fiction requires us to rethink our own assumptions about gender, literary criticism, language, and society. As it does so, it points to the need to go beyond revising science fiction plots to revising the way such stories are told.

Notes

1. Russ's *Female Man* and Monique Wittig's *Les Guérillères* are two notable exceptions. These texts prepare for a more general and widespread interest in post-modern elements in the 1980s.

2. As McCaffery explains, "SF writers share with their postmodernist cousins a sense of urgency about the need to reexamine central narrative assumptions and metaphorical frameworks" (6).

3. Janet Flax states that, "as a type of post-modern philosophy, feminist theory reveals and contributes to the growing uncertainty within Western intellectual circles about the appropriate grounding and methods for explaining and/or interpreting human experience" (624).

4. As McHale describes it, "science fiction, like post-modernist fiction, is governed by the ontological dominant. Indeed it is perhaps *the* ontological genre *par excellence*" (59).

5. Many works of feminist science fiction provide the synthesis of feminist and poststructuralist theory that Chris Weedon calls for in *Feminist Practice and Poststructuralist Theory*.

6. For example, Stanislaw Lem's diatribes against American popular science fiction in *Microworlds* are typical of critics who dismiss popular genres as simplistic.

7. Similar texts include Elgin's *Native Tongue* (1984), Marti Steussy's *Dreams of Dawn* (1988), and Susanna Sturgis's edited collection *Memories and Visions* (1989).

8. See, for example, Lessing's Canopus in Argos series (1979–83), Christine Brooke-Rose's *Xorander* (1986), Jody Scott's *I, Vampire* (1984), and Russ's *(Extra)ordinary People* (1984).

9. Examples of this type of text include: Anderson's *Virgin Planet*, Parley J. Cooper's *Feminists*, Robert W. Chambers's *Gay Rebellion*, and Thomas Berger's *Regiment of Women*. For a discussion of the texts, see Russ, *"Amor Vincit Foeminam."*

10. Le Guin identifies Gilligan's *In a Different Voice* as a work of great importance to her. She calls it "one of the most useful guides into the difficult area of cultural determination and enforcement of difference between male and female perception" (*Dancing* 20). On the subject of women writers, Le Guin says, "My understanding of this issue has been much aided by Carol Gilligan's *In a Different Voice*" (*Dancing* 231n).

WORKS CITED

Abbott, Edwin. *Flatland*. 1884. New York: Dover, 1952.

Ahearn, Marie. "Science Fiction in the Mainstream Novel." *Extrapolation* 20 (1979): 355–67.

Albinski, Nan Bowman. " 'The Laws of Justice, of Nature, and of Right': Victorian Feminist Utopias." *Feminism, Utopia, and Narrative*. Ed. Libby Falk Jones and Sarah Webster Goodwin. Knoxville: University of Tennessee Press, 1990.

———. *Women's Utopias in British and American Fiction*. New York: Routledge, 1988.

Aldiss, Brian. *Hothouse*. New York: Granada Publishers, 1979.

Andersen, Hans Christian. "The Snow Queen." *Stories from Hans Andersen*. New York: Abaris, 1979.

Anderson, Poul. *Virgin Planet*. 1959. New York: Warner, 1970.

Asimov, Isaac. *The Early Asimov*. New York: Doubleday, 1972.

Atwood, Margaret. *The Handmaid's Tale*. Boston: Houghton Mifflin, 1986.

Auerbach, Nina. *Communities of Women*. Cambridge: Harvard University Press, 1978.

———. *Woman and the Demon*. Cambridge: Harvard University Press, 1982.

Badami, Mary Kay. "A Feminist Critique of Science Fiction." *Extrapolation* 18 (December 1976): 6–19.

Baldick, Chris. *In Frankenstein's Shadow: Myth, Monstrosity, and Nineteenth-Century Writing*. Clarendon: Oxford University Press, 1987.

Bammer, Angelika. "Utopian Futures and Cultural Myopia." *Alternative Futures* 4 (1981): 3–17.

Barr, Marleen. *Alien to Femininity: Speculative Fiction and Feminist Theory*. New York: Greenwood Press, 1987.

Bartkowski, Frances. *Feminist Utopias*. Lincoln: University of Nebraska Press, 1989.

Bazin, Nancy Topping. "British Reviews of *Shikasta*." *Doris Lessing Newsletter* 4 (Winter 1980): 7, 9–15.

Beauvoir, Simone de. *The Second Sex*. 1952. New York: Vintage Books, 1974.

Bellamy, Edward. *Looking Backward*. 1888. New York: New American Library, 1960.

Benson, Edwin. "A World He Never Made." *Amazing Stories* 25 (1951): 8–55.

Beresford, J. O. *Goslings.* London: William Heinemann Co., 1913.

Berger, Thomas. *Regiment of Women.* New York: Simon and Schuster, 1973.

Bergonzi, Bernard. "The Time Machine: An Ironic Myth." *H. G. Wells: A Collection of Critical Essays.* Ed. Bernard Bergonzi. Englewood Cliffs, N.J.: Prentice Hall, 1976.

Besant, Walter. *The Revolt of Man.* London: Blackwood, 1882.

Brackett, Leigh. "Black Amazon of Mars." *Planet Stories* 4 (1951): 72–108.

Bradley, Marion Zimmer. *The Shattered Chain.* New York: DAW Books, 1976.

Bretnor, Reginald. "The Place of Science Fiction." *Modern Science Fiction.* New York: Coward McCann, 1953.

Brooke-Rose, Christine. *Xorander.* New York: Avon Books, 1988.

Brownmiller, Susan. *Against Our Will.* New York: Simon and Schuster, 1975.

Bryant, Dorothy. *The Kin of Ata Are Waiting for You.* 1971. New York: Random House, 1975.

Bucknall, Barbara. *Ursula K. Le Guin.* New York: Frederick Ungar, 1981.

Bullock, C. J., and Kay L. Stewart. "Post-Party Politics: Doris Lessing's Novels of the Seventies." *Massachusetts Review* 20 (1979): 245–57.

Bulwer-Lytton, Edward G. *The Coming Race.* Philadelphia: John Wanamaker, 1871.

Butler, Octavia. *Mind of My Mind.* New York: Avon Books, 1977.

———. *Wild Seed.* New York: Popular Library, 1980.

Byrd, Deborah. "A Permanent Escape from the Underworld: Doris Lessing's Use of the Demeter/Kore Myth in *Marriages between Zones Three, Four, and Five.*" Paper given at the Mid-Hudson MLA meeting, Poughkeepsie, N.Y., November 23, 1983.

Carter, Paul A. *The Creation of Tomorrow: Fifty Years of Magazine Science Fiction.* New York: Columbia University Press, 1977.

Chambers, Robert W. *The Gay Rebellion.* 1913. New York: Arno Press, 1974.

Chapman, Edgar L. "Sex, Satire and Feminism in the Science Fiction of Suzette Haden Elgin." *The Feminine Eye.* New York: Ungar, 1982.

Charnas, Suzy McKee. *Motherlines.* New York: Berkley, 1978.

———. "No Such Thing as Tearing Down Just a Little: Post-Holocaust Themes in Feminist SF." *Janus* 6 (1980): 25–28.

———, with Douglas E. Winter. "Mostly, I Want to Break Your Heart." *Fantasy Review* 7 (1984): 6–17.

Cherryh, C. J. "Cassandra." *Nebula Winners Fourteen.* Ed. Frederick Pohl. New York: Bantam, 1982.

———. *Hestia.* New York: DAW Books, 1979.

———. Introduction. *Lore of Witch World.* New York: DAW Books, 1980.

Chodorow, Nancy. *The Reproduction of Mothering.* Berkeley: University of California Press, 1978.

Cixous, Hélène. "The Laugh of the Medusa." *New French Feminisms.* Ed. Elaine Marks and Isabelle de Courtivan. New York: Schocken, 1981.

————, and Catherine Clément. *The Newly Born Woman.* Trans. Betsy Wing. Minneapolis: University of Minnesota Press, 1986.

Clareson, Thomas. "Lost Worlds, Lost Races: A Pagan Princess of Their Very Own." *Many Futures, Many Worlds.* Ed. Thomas Clareson. Kent State: Kent State University Press, 1977.

Collins, Jim. *Uncommon Cultures: Popular Culture and Postmodernism.* New York: Routledge, 1989.

Conklin, Groff, ed. *The Classic Book of Science Fiction.* New York: Bonanza, 1950.

Cooper, Parley J. *The Feminists.* New York: Pinnacle, 1971.

Day, Phyllis J. "Earthmother/Witchmother: Feminism and Ecology Renewed." *Extrapolation* 23 (1982): 12–21.

Del Rey, Lester. *The World of Science Fiction.* New York: Ballantine, 1979.

Derrida, Jacques. "The Ends of Man." *Philosophy and Phenomological Research* 30 (1969): 31–57.

De View, Lucille. Review of *The Making of the Representative for Planet 8* by Doris Lessing. *Christian Science Monitor* 7 January 1981: 17.

Dijkstra, Bram. *Idols of Perversity.* Oxford: Oxford University Press, 1986.

Donawerth, Jane. "Utopian Science: Contemporary Feminist Science Theory and Science Fiction by Women." *National Women's Studies Association Journal* 2 (1990): 535–57.

DuPlessis, Rachel Blau. "The Feminist Apologues of Lessing, Piercy and Russ." *Frontiers* 4 (1979): 1–8.

Ehrenreich, Barbara, and Deirdre English. *Witches, Midwives, Nurses.* Old Westbury, N.Y.: The Feminist Press, 1973.

Elgin, Suzette Haden. *And Then There'll Be Fireworks.* New York: Berkley Books, 1983.

————. *Communipath Worlds.* New York: Pocket Books, 1980.

————. *The Grand Jubilee.* New York: Berkley Books, 1983.

————. *The Judas Rose.* New York: DAW Books, 1987.

————. *Native Tongue.* New York: DAW Books, 1984.

————. *Star Anchored, Star Angered.* New York: Doubleday, 1979.

————. *Twelve Fair Kingdoms.* New York: Berkley Books, 1983.

Ellison, Harlan. "A Boy and His Dog." *Nebula Award Stories 5.* Ed. James Blish. New York: Doubleday, 1970.

Fairman, Paul W. "Invasion from the Deep." *Fantastic Adventures* 13 (1951): 6–47.

Farmer, Philip José. "The Lovers." *Startling Stories* 27 (1952): 12–63.

————. "Mother." 1953. *Modern Masterpieces of Science Fiction.* Ed. Sam Moskowitz. Cleveland: World Publishing Co., 1965.

Finch, Sheila. *Triad.* New York: Bantam, 1986.

Fishburn, Katherine. "Doris Lessing's *Briefing for a Descent into Hell:* Science Fiction or Psycho-Drama." *Science-Fiction Studies* 44 (1988): 48–60.

————. *The Unexpected Universe of Doris Lessing*. Westport, Conn.: Greenwood, 1985.

Flax, Janet. "Postmodernism and Gender Relations in Feminist Theory." *Signs* 12 (1987): 621–43.

Foster, Frances Smith. "Octavia Butler's Black Female Future Fiction." *Extrapolation* 23 (1982): 37–49.

Freibert, Lucy M. "World Views in Utopian Novels by Women." *Women and Utopia*. Ed. Marleen Barr and Nicholas O. Smith. New York: University Press of America, 1983.

Friedan, Betty. *The Feminine Mystique*. New York: Dell, 1963.

Friend, Beverly. "Virgin Territory: Women and Sex in Science Fiction." *Extrapolation* 14 (December 1972): 49–58.

Gilbert, Sandra, and Susan Gubar. *The Madwoman in the Attic*. New Haven: Yale University Press, 1979.

Gilligan, Carol. *In a Different Voice*. Cambridge: Harvard University Press, 1982.

Gilman, Charlotte Perkins. *Herland*. 1915. New York: Pantheon, 1979.

————. *The Yellow Wallpaper*. New York: The Feminist Press, 1973.

Gomoll, Jeanne. "Out of Context: Post-Holocaust Themes in Feminist Science Fiction." *Janus* 6 (1980): 14–17.

Gornick, Vivian. *Women in Science* New York: Touchstone, 1983.

Griffin, Susan. *Woman and Nature*. New York: Harper and Row, 1978.

Gunn, James. *Alternate Worlds*. Englewood Cliffs, N.J.: Prentice Hall, 1975.

Haggard, H. Rider. *She*. 1887. London: Octopus Books, 1979.

Hamilton, Edith. *Mythology*. New York: Mentor, 1942.

Haraway, Donna. "Animal Sociology and a Natural Economy of the Body Politic. Part I: A Political Physiology of Dominance." *Signs* 4 (1978); reprinted in *Sex and Scientific Inquiry*. Ed. Sandra Harding and Jean F. O'Barr. Chicago: University of Chicago Press, 1987.

————. *Primate Visions: Gender, Race, and Nature in the World of Modern Science*. New York: Routledge, 1989.

————. "Primatology Is Politics by Other Means." *Feminist Approaches to Science*. New York: Pergamon, 1986.

Harding, Sandra. *The Science Question in Feminism*. Ithaca: Cornell University Press, 1986.

Hazleton, Lesley. "Doris Lessing on Feminism, Communism, and 'Space Fiction.' " *New York Times Sunday Magazine* 25 July 1982: 20–21.

Heilbrun, Carolyn. *Reinventing Womanhood*. New York: W. W. Norton, 1979.

————. *Toward a Recognition of Androgyny*. New York: Harper and Row, 1973.

Herbert, Frank. *Dune*. 1965. New York: Berkley Publishing, 1980.

Huntington, John. *The Logic of Fantasy: H. G. Wells and Science Fiction*. New York: Columbia University Press, 1982.

Irigaray, Luce. "Is the Subject of Science Sexed?" *Cultural Critique* 1 (1985): 73–88.

————. *This Sex Which Is Not One.* Trans. Catherine Porter, with Carolyn Burke. Ithaca: Cornell University Press, 1985.

Jackson, Rosemary. *Fantasy: The Literature of Subversion.* New York: Methuen, 1981.

Jacobs, Naomi. "Beyond Stasis and Symmetry: Lessing, Le Guin, and the Remodeling of Utopia." *Extrapolation* 29 (1988): 33–45.

Johnson, Barbara. "My Monster/My Self." In *Mary Shelley's Frankenstein.* Ed. Harold Bloom. New York: Chelsea House, 1987.

Jones, Libby Falk, and Sarah Webster Goodwin, eds. *Feminism, Utopia, and Narrative.* Knoxville: University of Tennessee Press, 1990.

Keller, Evelyn Fox. *Reflections on Gender and Science.* New Haven: Yale University Press, 1985.

Kemp, Peter. *H. G. Wells and the Culminating Ape.* New York: St. Martin's Press, 1982.

Kessler, Carol Farley. Introduction. *Daring to Dream.* Boston: Pandora, 1984.

Ketterer, David. *New Worlds for Old.* New York: Anchor, 1974.

Khanna, Lee Cullen. "Women's Utopias: New Worlds, New Texts." *Feminism, Utopia, and Narrative.* Ed. Libby Falk Jones and Sarah Webster Goodwin. Knoxville: University of Tennessee Press, 1990.

————. "Women's Worlds: New Directions in Utopian Fiction." *Alternative Futures* 4 (Spring/Summer 1981): 47–60.

————. "Truth and Art in Women's Worlds: Doris Lessing's *Marriages between Zones Three, Four, and Five.*" *Women and Utopia.* Ed. Marleen Barr and Nicholas O. Smith. New York: University Press of America, 1983.

Kolodny, Annette. "Dancing through the Minefield: Some Observations on the Theory, Practice, and Politics of a Feminist Literary Criticism." *The New Feminist Criticism.* Ed. Elaine Showalter. New York: Pantheon, 1985.

Kristeva, Julia. *Powers of Horror: An Essay on Abjection.* New York: Columbia University Press, 1982.

Kuhn, Annette. *The Power of the Image.* Boston: Routledge, 1985.

Lake, Hugh J., Jr., ed. *The Last Man.* Mary Shelley. Lincoln: University of Nebraska Press, 1965.

Lane, Mary E. Bradley. *Mizora: A Prophecy.* 1890. Boston: Gregg Press, 1975.

LeClair, Tom. *The Art of Excess: Mastery in Contemporary American Fiction.* Urbana: University of Illinois Press, 1989.

Lee, Tanith. *The Silver Metal Lover.* New York: DAW Books, 1981.

Lefanu, Sarah. *Feminism and Science Fiction.* Bloomington: Indiana University Press, 1989.

Le Guin, Ursula K. *Always Coming Home.* New York: Harper and Row, 1985.

————. "American SF and the Other." *The Language of the Night.* New York: Putnam's, 1979.

————. *Dancing on the Edge of the World.* New York: Grove, 1989.

————. *The Dispossessed.* New York: Harper and Row, 1974.

————. *The Language of the Night.* New York: Putnam's, 1979.

————. *The Left Hand of Darkness.* 1969. New York: Ace Books, 1976.

————. *Rocannon's World.* New York: Ace Books, 1966.

————. "Science Fiction and Mrs. Brown." *The Language of the Night.* New York: Putnam's, 1979.

————. "Sur." *The Compass Rose.* New York: Bantam Books, 1983.

Lem, Stanislaw. *Microworlds.* New York: Harcourt, 1984.

Lessing, Doris. *Briefing for a Descent into Hell.* New York: Alfred A. Knopf, 1971.

————. *The Four-Gated City.* 1969. New York: Bantam Books, 1980.

————. *The Golden Notebook.* 1962. New York: Bantam Books, 1981.

————. *The Making of the Representative for Planet 8.* New York: Alfred A. Knopf, 1983.

————. *The Marriages between Zones Three, Four, and Five.* New York: Vintage Books, 1981.

————. *The Memoirs of a Survivor.* New York: Bantam Books, 1976.

————. "Report on a Threatened City." *The Temptation of Jack Orkney and Other Stories.* New York: Alfred A. Knopf, 1972.

————. *The Sentimental Agents.* New York: Alfred A. Knopf, 1983.

————. *Shikasta.* New York: Vintage Books, 1979.

————. *The Sirian Experiments.* New York: Vintage Books, 1980.

————. "To Room 19." *Stories.* New York: Alfred A. Knopf, 1978.

Lewontin, R. C., Steven Rose, and Leon J. Kamin. *Not in Our Genes.* New York: Pantheon, 1986.

Lowe, Marian. "Social Bodies: The Interaction of Culture and Women's Biology." *Biological Women: The Convenient Myth.* Cambridge, Mass.: Schenkman, 1982.

Lyotard, Jean-François. *The Postmodern Condition.* Trans. Geoff Bennington and Brian Massumi. Minneapolis: University of Minnesota Press, 1984.

McCaffery, Larry, ed. *Across the Wounded Galaxies: Interviews with Contemporary American Science Fiction Writers.* Urbana: University of Illinois Press, 1990.

McCaffrey, Anne. *The Ship Who Sang.* New York: Ballantine Books, 1969.

McHale, Brian. *Postmodernist Fiction.* New York: Methuen, 1987.

McIntyre, Vonda. *Dreamsnake.* London: Pan, 1979.

————. *Starfarers.* New York: Ace Books, 1989.

Maine, Charles Eric. *World without Men.* New York: Ace Books, 1958.

May, Julian. *The Adversary.* Boston: Houghton Mifflin Co., 1984.

————. *The Golden Torc.* Boston: Houghton Mifflin Co., 1982.

————. *The Many-Colored Land.* Boston: Houghton Mifflin Co., 1980.

————. *The Nonborn King.* Boston: Houghton Mifflin Co., 1981.

Mellor, Anne K. *Mary Shelley: Her Life, Her Fiction, Her Monsters.* New York: Methuen, 1988.

Miner, Madonne M. "Guaranteed to Please: Twentieth-Century American Women's

Bestsellers." *Gender and Reading.* Ed. Elizabeth A. Flynn and Patricinio Schweickart. Baltimore: Johns Hopkins University Press, 1986.

Moers, Ellen. *Literary Women.* New York: Anchor, 1977.

Monk, Patricia. "Frankenstein's Daughters: The Problem of Feminine Image in SF." *Mosaic* 13 (Spring/Summer 1980): 15–27.

Montagu, Ashley. *The Natural Superiority of Women.* 1952. New York: MacMillan, 1968.

Morgan, Ellen. "Alienation of the Woman Writer in *The Golden Notebook.*" *Doris Lessing: Critical Studies.* Madison: University of Wisconsin Press, 1973.

Morgan, Robin. *Going Too Far.* New York: Vintage Books, 1977.

Morris, Meaghan. *The Pirate's Fiancée: Feminism, Reading, and Postmodernism.* New York: Verso, 1988.

Moskowitz, Sam. *Strange Horizons.* New York: Scribner's, 1976.

———, ed. *When Women Rule.* New York: Walker Publishing Co., 1972.

Neumann, Erich. *The Great Mother.* 1955. Princeton: Princeton University Press, 1972.

Neville, Kris. "The Opal Necklace." *Fantastic* 1 (Summer 1953): 76–89.

Nicholls, Peter, ed. *The Science Fiction Encyclopedia.* New York: Doubleday, 1979.

Niven, Larry. *Ringworld.* New York: Ballantine, 1970.

Norton, Andre. *Ordeal in Otherwhere.* 1964. Boston: Gregg Press, 1980.

———. *Witch World.* 1963. New York: Ace Books, 1983.

"No Such Thing as Tearing Down Just a Little: Transcription of a Panel Discussion of NoreasCon 2." *Janus* 6 (1980): 16–27.

O'Brien, Geoffrey. *Hardboiled America.* New York: Von Nostrand Reinhold, 1981.

O'Flinn, Paul. "Production and Reproduction: The Case of *Frankenstein.*" In *Popular Fictions.* Ed. Peter Humm, Paul Stigant, and Peter Widdowson. New York: Methuen, 1986.

Parrinder, Patrick. "Descents into Hell: The Later Novels of Doris Lessing." *Critical Quarterly* 22 (1980): 7–19.

———, ed. *H. G. Wells: The Critical Heritage.* Boston: Routledge and Kegan Paul, 1972.

Patai, Daphne. "Beyond Defensiveness: Feminist Research Strategies." *Women and Utopia.* Ed. Marleen Barr and Nicholas O. Smith. New York: University Press of America, 1983.

Pearson, Carol. "Women's Fantasies and Feminist Utopias." *Frontiers* 2 (1973): 48–65.

Pfaelzer, Jean. *The Utopian Novel in America, 1886–1896: The Politics of Form.* Pittsburgh: University of Pittsburgh Press, 1984.

Philmus, Robert M. *Into the Unknown.* Berkeley: University of California Press, 1970.

Piercy, Marge. *Woman on the Edge of Time.* New York: Fawcett, 1976.

Pizan, Christine de. *The Book of the City of Ladies.* Trans. Earl Jeffrey Richards. 1405. New York: Persea Books, 1982.

Platt, Charles. *Dream Makers, Volume 2.* New York: Berkley Books, 1983.

Podojil, Catherine. "Sisters, Daughters, and Aliens." *Critical Encounters.* New York: Ungar, 1978.

Pournelle, Jerry, ed. *Nebula Award Stories.* New York: Holt, Rhinehart, and Winston, 1982.

Pratt, Annis. *Archetypal Patterns in Women's Fiction.* Bloomington: Indiana University Press, 1981.

Rhodes, Jewel P. "Ursula K. Le Guin's *The Left Hand of Darkness:* Androgyny and the Feminist Utopian Vision." *Women and Utopia.* Ed. Marleen Barr and Nicholas O. Smith. New York: University Press of America, 1983.

Rich, Adrienne. *Of Woman Born.* New York: Bantam, 1977.

Rigney, Barbara Hill. *Madness and Sexual Politics in the Feminist Novel.* Madison: University of Wisconsin Press, 1978.

Rose, Mark. *Alien Encounters.* Cambridge: Harvard University Press, 1981.

Rosinky, Natalie. *Feminist Futures: Contemporary Women's Speculative Fiction.* Ann Arbor: University Microfilms International Research Press, 1984.

Rothstein, Mervyn. "No Balm in Gilead for Margaret Atwood." *New York Times* 12 February 1986: C11.

Rowe, Karen. "Feminism and Fairy Tales." *Women's Studies* 6 (1979): 237–57.

Rubenstein, Roberta. *The Novelistic Vision of Doris Lessing.* Urbana: University of Illinois Press, 1979.

Russ, Joanna. "*Amor Vincit Foeminam:* The Battle of the Sexes in Science Fiction." *Science-Fiction Studies* 7 (1980): 2–15.

———. *(Extra)ordinary People.* New York: St. Martin's Press, 1984.

———. *The Female Man.* New York: Bantam, 1978.

———. "Recent Feminist Utopias." *Future Females: A Critical Anthology.* Ed. Marleen S. Barr. Bowling Green: Bowling Green University Press, 1981.

———. "When It Changed." *The New Women of Wonder.* Ed. Pamela Sargent. New York: Vintage Books, 1978.

Sanders, Scott. "Woman as Nature in Science Fiction." *Future Females: A Critical Anthology.* Ed. Marleen S. Barr. Bowling Green: Bowling Green University Press, 1981.

Sargent, Pamela. *The Shore of Women.* New York: Bantam Books, 1987.

———, ed. *More Women of Wonder.* New York: Vintage Books, 1976.

Saxton, Ruth. "Lessing in California, April 5–10." *Doris Lessing Newsletter* 8 (Fall 1984): 7.

Schlobin, Roger C. "Andre Norton: Humanity amid the Hardware." *The Feminine Eye.* New York: Ungar, 1982.

Schmitz, James. *The Witches of Karres.* 1966. New York: Ace, 1982.

Schweickart, Patricinio. "What If . . . : Science and Technology in Feminist Utopias." *Machina Ex Dea.* Ed. Joan Rothschild. New York: Pergamon, 1983.

Scott, Jody. *I, Vampire.* New York: Ace Books, 1984.

Segal, Howard P. "The Feminist Technological Utopia: Mary E. Bradley Lane's *Mizora* (1890)." *Alternative Futures* 4 (Spring/Summer 1981): 67–72.

Shaver, Richard S. "The Fall of Lemuria." *Other Worlds* (November 1949): 4–41.

Shelley, Mary. *Frankenstein; or, The Modern Prometheus.* 1831. New York: Signet, 1965.

———. *The Last Man.* 1826. Lincoln: University of Nebraska Press, 1965.

Shelton, Robert. "Themes of the Other in Canopus: Reading Lessing with Stapledon and Clarke." Paper given at the Modern Language Association meeting, New York, N.Y., 31 December 1983.

Shinn, Thelma. *Worlds within Women.* New York: Greenwood, 1986.

Showalter, Elaine. "Feminist Criticism in the Wilderness." *Critical Inquiry* 8 (1981): 187–202.

Slonczewski, Joan. *A Door into Ocean.* New York: Avon, 1986.

Somay, Bulent. "Toward an Open-ended Utopia." *Science-Fiction Studies* 11 (1984): 25–38.

Stamberg, Susan. "An Interview with Doris Lessing." *Doris Lessing Newsletter* 8 (1984): 3–4, 15.

Steussy, Marti. *Dreams of Dawn.* New York: Ballantine Books, 1988.

Stitzell, Judith. "Reading Doris Lessing." *College English* 40 (1979): 498–504.

Sturgeon, Theodore. *Venus Plus X.* 1960. Boston: Gregg Press, 1976.

Sturgis, Susanna, ed. *Memories and Visions: Women's Fantasy and Science Fiction.* Freedom, Calif.: Crossing Press, 1989.

Suter, Jaquelyn, and Sandy Flitterman. "Textual Riddles: Woman as Enigma or Site of Social Meanings? An Interview with Laura Mulvey." *Discourse* 1 (Fall 1979): 86–127.

Suvin, Darko. *Metamorphoses of Science Fiction.* New Haven: Yale University Press, 1979.

———. *Victorian Science Fiction.* Boston: G. K. Hall, 1983.

Tenneshaw, S. M. "Queen of the Ice Men." *Fantastic* 11 (November 1949): 8–32; reprinted in ibid. 8 (Spring 1950): 8–32.

Tepper, Sheri. *The Gate to Women's Country.* New York: Bantam Books, 1989.

Thornburg, Mary R. Patterson. *The Monster in the Mirror: Gender and the Sentimental/Gothic Myth in Frankenstein.* Ann Arbor: University of Michigan Press, 1987.

Tiger, Virginia. "Candid Shot." *Doris Lessing Newsletter* 8 (Fall 1984): 5.

Tiptree, James, Jr. *Up the Walls of the World.* New York: Ace, 1984.

Turkle, Sherry. *The Second Self.* New York: Simon and Schuster, 1984.

Turner, A. K. Review of *The Making of the Representative for Planet 8* by Doris Lessing. *Nation* 6 March 1982: 234, 278.

Van Syoc, Sydney J. *Darkchild.* New York: Berkley Books, 1982.

Veeder, William. *Mary Shelley and Frankenstein: The Fate of Androgyny.* Chicago: University of Chicago Press, 1986.

Vinge, Joan D. *Psion*. New York: Delacorte Press, 1982.

——. *The Snow Queen*. New York: Dial Press, 1980.

——. *World's End*. New York: Bluejay, 1984.

Waugh, Patricia. *Feminine Fiction: Revisitng the Postmodern*. New York: Routledge, 1989.

Weedon, Chris. *Feminist Practice and Poststructuralist Theory*. New York: Basil Blackwell, 1987.

Wells, H. G. *The Complete Science Fiction Treasury of H. G. Wells*. 1895. New York: Avenel, 1978.

Weston, George. *His First Million Women*. New York: Farrar and Rinehart, 1934.

Wittig, Monique. *Les Guérillières*. 1969. Boston: Beacon Press, 1971.

Wylie, Philip. *The Disappearance*. New York: Rinehart and Co., 1951.

Zoline, Pamela. "The Heat Death of the Universe." *The New Women of Wonder*. Ed. Pamela Sargent. New York: Vintage Books, 1977.

Index

ROBIN ROBERTS has a Ph.D. from the University of Pennsylvania and is an assistant professor in the Department of English at Louisiana State University. She is the author of articles in the *NWSA Journal, Extrapolation,* the *Journal of Popular Culture,* and *Science-Fiction Studies,* among others.